VIRGINIA'S HAUNTED HISTORIC TRIANGLE

Williamsburg, Yorktown, Jamestown,
& Other Haunted Locations

PAMELA K. KINNEY

4880 Lower Valley Road, Atglen, Pennsylvania 19310

DEDICATION

To Hans Holzer and L. B. Taylor…

† Hans Holzer's ghost books were the first ones I ever read. He traveled and recorded fabulous stories of hauntings in many parts of the world.

† When I moved to Virginia, it was L. B. Taylor's *The Ghosts of Williamsburg and Nearby Environs* that was my first introduction to his marvelous ghost books of Virginia.

Schiffer Books are available at special discounts for bulk purchases for sales promotions or premiums. Special editions, including personalized covers, corporate imprints, and excerpts can be created in large quantities for special needs. For more information contact the publisher:

Published by Schiffer Publishing Ltd.
4880 Lower Valley Road
Atglen, PA 19310
Phone: (610) 593-1777; Fax: (610) 593-2002
E-mail: Info@schifferbooks.com

For the largest selection of fine reference books on this and related subjects,
please visit our website at: **www.schifferbooks.com**
We are always looking for people to write books on new and related subjects.
If you have an idea for a book please contact us at the above address.

This book may be purchased from the publisher.
Include $5.00 for shipping.
Please try your bookstore first.
You may write for a free catalog.

In Europe, Schiffer books are distributed by
Bushwood Books
6 Marksbury Ave.
Kew Gardens
Surrey TW9 4JF England
Phone: 44 (0) 20 8392 8585; Fax: 44 (0) 20 8392 9876
E-mail: info@bushwoodbooks.co.uk
Website: www.bushwoodbooks.co.uk

Other Schiffer Books by the Author:
Haunted Virginia, 978-0-7643-3281-4, $14.99
Haunted Richmond, 978-0-7643-2712-4, $14.95

Other Schiffer Books on Related Subjects:
Ghosts of Bridgewater Triangle, 978-0-7643-3006-3, $14.99
Haunted Battlefields: Virginia's Civil War Ghosts, 978-0-7643-3057-5, $14.99
Haunted Plantations of Virginia, 978-0-7643-3228-6, $14.99
Ghosts, Legends, and Lore of Hampton Roads, 978-0-7643-3426-9, $14.99

Copyright © 2011 by Pamela K. Kinney
Unless otherwise noted, all images are the property of the author.
Library of Congress Control Number: 2011926453

Designed by Mark David Bowyer
Type set in DeRoos / NewBaskerville BT

ISBN: 978-0-7643-3746-8
Printed in China

CONTENTS

ACKNOWLEDGMENTS

I would like to thank and acknowledge my husband, Bill, for being patient with me again as I worked on this book. He acted as my assistant and drove me to many of the places to check them out and take photographs. I like to acknowledge my son, Chris, for he loves reading true ghost stories and stayed to the end of "Ghost Adventures" late Halloween night when I went to bed so he could let me know the ending.

I thank, Alexa Day, my critique person for this book. Without you, girlfriend, this book just wouldn't be!

I also would like to definitely thank my great editors, Dinah Roseberry and Jennifer Marie Savage. Without their supreme expertise, this book would have never found its way to the shelves of bookstores, museums, libraries, and private owners.

I thank Julian Charity, Janet L. Appel, and Randy Carter of the Shirley Plantation, Dot Boulware of the Edgewood Plantation, and Kathryn Hulick of the Boxwood Inn. These wonderful people let me into these superb places and let me know all about their ghosts.

I would also like to thank Berkeley Plantation, Jamestown, Colonial Williamsburg, Yorktown, Fort Monroe, and the National Parks, City of Newport News, City of Hampton, Rosewell Foundation, Blue Gap Farm, and many of the numerous groups that kept these places from being torn down for condominiums and apartments. It's not just about the ghosts, but also the history you kept from being lost.

I also thank Patty Ceran and the other witnesses, along with the paranormal investigators of RTL, who shared their experiences with me to be put in this book.

INTRODUCTION

"By the pricking of my thumbs,
Something wicked this way comes.
Open, locks,
Whoever knocks!"
— William Shakespeare

History has a way of causing hauntings. There are intelligent ones and residuals that seem to repeat over and over. Ghostly soldiers are seen fighting in Civil War and Revolutionary War battlefields till this day. Suddenly, parties or balls from the past appeared for a few minutes in ballrooms in plantations or in taverns. Some people can't seem to let go of a house they no longer own even though they've been dead and gone for a century or two. Those who rent a room for the night at a hotel or a bed and breakfast might wake up to find someone in bed with them, trying to steal a kiss. And I am not talking about someone who walked into their room by mistake, but someone who suddenly vanishes into thin air. Even a park can be the scene of a paranormal event. Not all hauntings are caused by those long gone. Ghosts of a person, who just passed away, can haunt a place — like a dental office!

I jumped at the opportunity to do this book set in the Historic Triangle — it would give me the chance to check out some of the great places I had only read about or never been to and revisit places I hadn't been to for a long time. Not only did I investigate Williamsburg, Yorktown, and Jamestown, but also Charles City (which has some super plantations), the railroad crossing where the famous Cohoke Light has been seen for years, haunts of Hampton, Newport News, and Gloucester, too. I am sure there are many more places I did not get to learn about or will find out about after this book has been published, but I discovered so many buildings and outdoor settings that had paranormal activity for years, if not centuries.

Not only did I find some great ghost stories and have experiences myself, but I learned history I never knew before — history that I hope others will find out by reading this book. After all, to know the history is to understand reasons for the hauntings. In addition to true hauntings, myths and urban legends are sprinkled throughout the chapters and I've also added Bigfoot and UFO sightings — they were just too cool not to include.

It was quite a feeling to be able to step onto Jamestown Island, where Captain John Smith and the first English colonists had the first colony. To follow in Smith's footsteps and see where he traveled and to get to see the very area where the Powhatan and Pocahontas lived was amazing. I got to walk in Yorktown, where some of the battles of the Revolutionary War were fought, and to maybe even trace the same footsteps of

Thomas Jefferson and George Washington as they walked along Duke of Gloucester Street. No matter where you turned, all that stuff in the history books actually happened! It was exciting!

The history was the bonus for the ghost stories. Some of that history came alive for me when I caught an odd noise or a voice on an EVP, or captured something out of the ordinary on my photos. I suspect the ghosts wanted to let me know their story. I pray I did justice to those tales in this book.

I just hope that after you read this book, you will want to go and check out these places. Colonial Williamsburg is history brought to life 365 days a year. Jamestown has archeological digs going on, and they'll be glad to tell you what they are doing and what they found so far. Those plantations in Charles City want you to visit them. Go to Yorktown and check out the buildings, the battleground, and Cornwallis's Cave. There's so much to see and do — and if you're lucky, you just might catch sight of a ghost or hear the soft whisper of a voice long gone or the boom from cannon fire.

Turn the page and step back into the past. Be prepared to get to know the ghosts of Virginia's Historic Triangle and its surrounding areas. They're dying for you to read their stories.

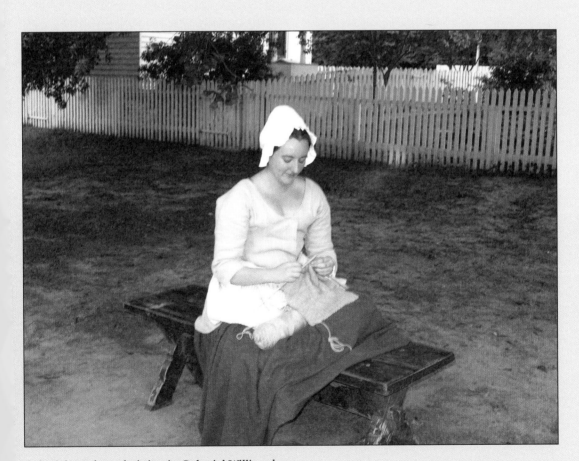

Colonial employee knitting in Colonial Williamsburg

Section One

HAUNTED HISTORIC TRIANGLE

Chapter One

WILLIAMSBURG

Williamsburg is quite a contradictory city. First, there are its history, ranging from Colonial to Revolutionary War to the Civil War, and afterwards. Not far away, in Charles City County, York County, and even in Williamsburg itself, are plantations one can visit. Jamestown (both the historical and the attraction version) is in nearby James City County. This is where John Smith helped establish the first English settlement in the New World and met Pocahontas. Battlefields of both the Revolution and War Between the States were fought in the Historic Triangle area. There are museums, along with Colonial Williamsburg and Historic Yorktown.

There's another side to Williamsburg too: a touristy one. Restaurants, outlet shopping centers, Busch Gardens, Water Country USA, theaters (like Haunted Dinner Theatre and Mystery Dinner Playhouse), plenty of ghost tours, President's Park, Ripley's Believe it or Not, art museums, a winery, a microbrewery, the College of William and Mary, Williamsburg Pottery, and Great Wolf Lodge. Once a year, in January, there's even a science fiction, fantasy, and horror convention, Marscon (www.marscon.net), held here. I've been a guest author for them for the past several years; before that, I attended it as a fan. As the various ghost tours indicate, Williamsburg also has attractions of the ghostly kind. A lot of it is all due to the history that permeates the area.

Williamsburg began life under the name "Middle Plantation." It was a fortified settlement located on high ground on the Peninsula between the James and York Rivers in the 1600s. It was renamed Williamsburg after the capital of the Virginia Colony moved there from Jamestown in 1698. The town received a royal charter as a city in 1722 and became the center of political events in Virginia leading to the American Revolution.

It is well known for Colonial Williamsburg, the restored historic section of the city, and the College of William & Mary, established in 1693. William and Mary is the second-oldest university in the United States, only beaten by Harvard University in Massachusetts. Nearby, established in 1770, lies the predecessor of the current Eastern State Hospital, the first known mental hospital in the United States.

Most highway travelers can reach Williamsburg via nearby Interstate 64, U.S. Route 60, and State Route 143. There's commercial airline services located at nearby Newport News/Williamsburg International Airport and the Richmond and Norfolk airports. All are located along I-64 and offer limousine service to Williamsburg, as well as rental cars. Amtrak and Greyhound, along with taxicabs and the local transit bus system makes it easy to get to the attractions and museums here. Many Virginia schools have used Colonial Williamsburg for field trips.

There are many hotels to choose from if you don't live in the area, and a variety of things to do once you settle in. You can buy a day pass or one that encompasses all year and visit Colonial Williamsburg. Of course, you don't need one of these to take the ghost tours, although Colonial Williamsburg is a very cool place to learn history. Taken out of the stuffy boredom of history books, you get to intermingle with workers dressed in costumes from the era. This is definitely a place where history comes alive. For more information, visit www.history.org.

Many of the taverns, public outbuildings, and homes are reproductions on their original foundations. Others are the original eighteenth century homes. The Historic Area covers just a bit over three hundred acres. Some of the buildings are open to the public. Others are private residences and administrative offices. A flag at a building's entrance indicates when a particular site is open. For most of those you can tour, each has at least one day it is closed to the public.

Once you catch the bus from the Visitor's Center and disembark near the Governor's Palace, you'll see there are no vehicles allowed on Duke of Gloucester Street. For delivery trucks to deliver goods and foodstuffs for the taverns there is an underground tunnel that leads from the kitchens beneath the taverns to buildings off Francis Street. My husband, Bill, and I used this tunnel late after the ghost tour we took to get from Shields Tavern kitchens to the parking lot on Francis Street where our car had been parked. One of the ghosts has been seen in this tunnel.

Many of the places were witness to political events. The Governor's Palace embodied British rule in the Colonies. The Capitol was where the vote for the move for independence happened. Raleigh Tavern held many debates. The Magazine was where they stored the colony's guns and ammunition.

The newest exhibit, a coffeehouse, just opened in November 2009. The place is not like the coffee shops of today. Owned by a wigmaker, Richard Carlton, this is where gentlemen came to discuss many things over cups of coffee, cocoa, or tea — where they made deals, did business, exchange gossip, or received news of England. One encounter that led to the Revolution happened on the front porch in 1765. An angry crowd protested the Stamp Act and confronted George Mercer, the appointed collector for Virginia. Lucky for Mercer, the royal governor of the time, Frances Fauquier, intervened. Mercer resigned from his post not long afterwards. As for the Stamp Act, the British Parliament repealed it later that year.

So you can see how these turbulent times could be a good basis for many of the hauntings in the area...just in Colonial Williamsburg alone. Of course that doesn't include Richmond Road, where phantom Civil War soldiers have been seen passing through many of the hotels that line the roadway. Ghostly occurrences have been reported in some of the hotels.

To start this journey into the ghostly realms of Williamsburg, let's begin with what I learned about the Historic Area of Williamsburg, thanks to the Tavern Ghost Walk (http://www.colonialwilliamsburg.com/visit/whatToSeeAndDo/activitiesAndPrograms/tavernghostwalk.cfm), from other books, and even from what I experienced myself. As you'll see, Colonial Williamsburg's spectral residents never really left.

HAUNTED ROADS

"There be those who say that things and places have souls, and there be those who say they have not; I dare not say, myself, but I will tell of The Street." — H. P. Lovecraft

Even though the Civil War has been over, there are Rebels still trying to get away from Northern troops. They had fled Yorktown and passed through Williamsburg to get to Richmond on May 3, 1862. Many died on these streets from starvation. Two roads in Williamsburg — Duke of Gloucester and Richmond Road — have had phantom sightings.

One home along the route had some mysterious goings-on, like someone walking though their house and a rocking chair just rocking away. One of their doors kept flying open, as did a freezer. All this time, their cats would watch something not there.

Just as quickly it all started, the events quit. Whatever had been in their home had left. Had it been a Confederate trying to get to Richmond who paused for a rest — or something else?

A part of Richmond Road.

Haunted Hotels

Those staying in hotels on Richmond Road tell of seeing soldiers passing through their rooms. One woman on a tour had turned white when she heard about this and told of her own experience. She had gone to get some ice and when she returned to the room, a Confederate soldier walked by her in the hall. He passed through the hotel wall and vanished!

Another couple staying in a hotel woke up to the sound of someone going through their suitcase. They lay there frightened. Then the husband turned on the light and they found clothing from the suitcases scattered across the floor.

Next time you stay at a hotel in Williamsburg and hear noises in your room at night, just ignore them and go back to sleep. It's just a soldier passing through on his way to Richmond.

Holiday Inn Patriot on Richmond Road where we stay for Marscon every year.

CIVIL WAR BATTLEFIELD

"It is well that war is so terrible. We should grow too fond of it." — Robert E. Lee

Williamsburg is more than Colonial times. Did you know that a Civil War battle was also fought here?

The Battle of Williamsburg was fought May 5, 1862. Also known as the Battle of Fort Magruder, it took place as part of the Peninsula Campaign. Casualties that included the cavalry skirmishing on May 4 were 1,682 Confederates and 2,283 Union of the nearly 41,000 Federals and 32,000 Confederates. A steady downpour of rain in the thick woods did not help much for either side. Ten hours of combat raged on. One wounded Union soldier managed to get three Rebel officers to a local prison. Townspeople under cover of umbrellas watched the battle.

When the Rebels retreated, they got caught up with local civilians. The civilians panicked and retreated. By nightfall, the Union won and General Joseph Johnston led the Confederates out of town to Richmond. Major General George McClellan telegraphed to Washington, "The victory is complete."

Wounded Confederate soldiers were still being found by the third day, and the dead were either half buried in mud or piled up high. Fire blazed on the third day in the woods, and those still alive died terribly.

Since the battle, houses have been built on the land, though some of it became a park. Though the war has been over for more than 148 years, it is still being fought.

Betty and Sam Littleton have a house on where the battle took place. When they first moved in, they woke up each night to the sounds of people running in their yard. A bloodstained face peered in their bedroom window and scared Betty. They heard horrific screams, moans, and sabers; all keeping them awake at night. When they sat in their living room, sounds of cannons and gunfire came to them. They even would watch some of the ghostly battle from their back porch. The spirit of one young Confederate soldier would be seen darting from tree to tree as if hiding from the enemy. One night the couple heard voices and then a snap of a rope as if someone had just been hanged!

The marker for the Battle of Williamsburg is located in Redoubt Park on Quarterpath Road, but don't be surprised if you don't hear sounds of a battle going on when you check out the area.

MORE THAN REST AT THIS WILLIAMSBURG HOTEL

Just like any other city, Williamsburg has taverns, bed and breakfasts, motels, and hotels, but, like the rest of the city, many have hauntings. Maybe just like such places in other cities and towns. It's just that Williamsburg has so much history a lot of the paranormal stuff could be an attributing factor.

One of these stories happened to Jackie Tomlin at Williamsburg's Hospitality House, across from the College of William and Mary. In the early 1990s, she worked for her father at his dealership, 360 Auto Sales, and he sent her to a convention for car dealers.

On her first night, she went out to dinner and then came back and went to bed at 9 p.m. At 9:30 p.m., she awoke to the sound of muttering outside her door and feet running back and forth in the hallway. She got up and peeked out, but found no one. She closed the door and went back to bed. Once again, the sound of children running back and forth in the hallway commenced. She checked again, looking out her door.

Nothing.

She went back to bed. The running kept up until 11:30 p.m. and then all was quiet for the rest of the night.

The second night of her stay, at 9:30, the children running back and forth in the hallway started up. This time, when she popped her head out the door, she saw another head pop out from another room two doors down. This was a man. Both went back into their rooms because there was nothing there. Thirty minutes later when the running happened again, they looked out again, and this time, Jackie and he talked about the phenomena. He hadn't been there the first night and she told him this had happened until 11:30 p.m. that night. They decided to go downstairs to the hotel desk to get some answers.

The young woman at the desk said, "I have no idea, but there have been others that have complained about the children running on that floor before." She went on to say that the entire hotel had been booked for the car convention people and that there were no children at all.

Whoever the ghostly children are, it seems that maybe with no adult supervision they could play at night when most children are asleep in bed.

COLLEGE OF WILLIAM AND MARY

"Imagination is more important than knowledge. Knowledge is limited.
Imagination encircles the world." — Albert Einstein.

Colleges are more than places of learning and higher education, and they have more than fraternity parties or football games. Sometimes they have ghosts — and even some urban legends that are passed from student to student over the years.

A female apparition has been seen over the years. It is said that is the ghost of Lucinda, a student who died in a car accident on the way to star in a play on campus, "Our Town."

The College of William and Mary is located at the far western end of Duke of Gloucester Street. The Wren Building faces Duke of Gloucester Street and the President's House is to its right.

Wren Building

The College of William and Mary is the second oldest college in the United States. Many great men attended here, including Thomas Jefferson. Thanks to James Blair, a charter to establish the school was granted by King William and Queen Mary in 1693, with the college's main building, the Wren Building, being constructed in 1695. It got its name from Sir Christopher Wren, an English architect. It is believed he designed the building.

The Wren Building

The House of Burgess met in Wren Building from 1700 to 1704. It was a makeshift hospital during the Revolutionary war. During 1812, the place was used as barracks for militia. Fires from 1705, 1859 and 1862 did damage to it and each time it was rebuilt it changed more and more. When Williamsburg was restored, they worked on the Wren Building to return it to its original facade before all the fires.

One of these fires happened when the Federal soldiers occupied Williamsburg. Drunk, some soldiers thought that Southern sharpshooters hid inside the Wren Building. They set the building ablaze and kept the townspeople at bay, refusing to let them try and save the place.

Two buildings were added in the eighteenth century, flanking the right and left of Wren Building; one was a chapel in 1732. Governor Botetourt, Sir John Randolph, and his two sons, Peyton and John, are entombed beneath its floor. The Brafferton was added in 1723.

Brafferton Hall

The Brafferton was used to educate Native American boys. Originally, the Indian boys were housed in nearby farms and houses. However, the boys experienced quite a bit of abuse and were exposed to English diseases, of which they had no immunity against. The Indian College first stopped in 1721, but it was revived when Brafferton Hall was built in 1723, using funds provided by the well-known scientist, Robert Boyle. The Indian boys were moved in there to live and learn their lessons. Separated from their families and homes, the boys were still unhappy and, since they came from several different nations,

Hallway on second floor of Brafferton Hall.

language was even a barrier between them. There is one story where an Indian boy was able to escape the hall at night, ran freely about the campus, and returned to the hall before dawn. One day, he was found dead. Some said that he had died of a 'broken heart.' Others say someone shot him. By 1736, Brafferton Hall was no longer used to house the Indians, and the Indian College was closed for good by 1779.

The ghost stories surrounding this place concern the beating of tom-toms heard throughout. People have also claimed seeing the ghost of the Indian boy racing about the building and campus. In areas that have been built up, his body is seen half-buried in the ground as he runs, mostly in the Sunken Garden. The legend goes that a misty night is the best time to catch sight of him.

Wilford Kale who was a bureau chief for the *Richmond Times-Dispatch*, worked at the college in the mid-1960s. He reported hearing footsteps on the third floor where he slept. He would check, but could never find the source of the sounds. On another occasion, he woke to the sound of rhythmic beating like on tom-toms. The sound went on for about a minute-and-a-half. There are also others who have reported sounds like feet shuffling and sobbing.

Used nowadays for administration offices, Brafferton Hall had previously served as a dormitory, a dining hall, a classroom, and a professor's residence. I toured Brafferton on May 19, 2010 and caught some orbs on photos. There was also an odd blur, but only at where the doorway leads into the hall that has all the portraits of the college presidents.

Couple of orbs in a section on second floor of Brafferton Hall.

Orb on floor.

Odd blur from doorway into the hallway with college presidents' portraits.

The President's House

The President's House was completed in 1733. All but one of the college's presidents lived there. The first to live there was James Blair. During the Revolutionary War, Cornwallis commandeered it. When the War Between the States began, the Confederates took it over as a storage facility and a hospital. After the Battle of Williamsburg, both Union and Rebel troops used the hospital, blood spilling onto the lawn. After the battle, the Union imprisoned Confederates within its walls.

Some of the strange things that occur at the President's House included windows that open and close by themselves, doors slamming shut, and an eerie feeling. Some think the ghosts are colonials; others say it's an unhappy bride. Maybe even those soldiers who died within its walls when it was a hospital?

The President's House on William and Mary Campus.

Tucker Hall

The story goes that some haunt visits students who choose to pull all-nighters in the classroom on the third floor of St. George Tucker Hall. The ghost's identity is unknown, as it has been rumored to be anyone ranging from a resident of Colonial Williamsburg during the Revolution to a disgruntled or suicidal student at the college.

Who haunts Tucker Hall?

Campus Legends

The following urban legend sounds somewhat like the urban legend surrounding the gazebo at the University of Richmond in my book *Haunted Virginia: Legends, Myths and True Tales*. Do college students pass this stuff around?

Crim Dell

There's an urban legend behind the Crim Dell Bridge that if you walk across its bridge with your significant other and kiss at the top, you are destined to marry that person and be in love forever. If you break-up, however, you will remain cursed unless one member of the hopeless couple pushes the other into the Crim Dell. It's never agreed upon as to who should be chucked over the edge — girls will say it's the boy who should be pushed, and boys will say it's the girl. Avoid walking across it alone, however, unless you want to be doomed to a life of loneliness.

Statue of Lord Botetourt

Another urban legend surrounds the statue of Lord Botetourt. It is said that if a student touches the statue, he or she will get a good grade on his or her next test.

Crim Dell.

Statue of Lord Botetourt.

TWO WILLIAMSBURG HAUNTINGS

The Ghost in Merchant's Square

Head toward the College of William and Mary down Duke of Gloucester Street, away from the Historic Area, and you'll find Merchant's Square. Bookstores, dining places, and shops are scattered across the area. Need a book, find it in the College of William and Mary Bookstore or Mermaid Books. Places to dine can be found from ice cream at Baskin Robbins to Seasons Restaurant. There are also shops of all kinds where you can find peanuts, toys, collectibles, and much, much more.

Henry Street Shops at Merchant Square.

Even more than a good shopping experience, though, there's a ghost still haunting the area. Where the Henry Street Shops now stand used to be where Horace Moore lived. When he answered the call to fight in the Civil War, he died in battle. His brother, Thomas Moore, inherited the house. The man loved wandering and the ladies on an equal status.

Thomas had become involved with a married woman who met him at the house in secret for their trysts. Except Harvey Hall, the cuckolded husband heard rumors that she met Thomas at his house and went there. He found his wife in the arms of her lover and grew angry. The men argued and, in the end, Thomas Moore ended dead.

Hall and his frightened wife hid the body in the basement, but the body was discovered eight days later. Hall went on trial and was convicted of Moore's murder and imprisoned for life. Shunned from all, Mrs. Hall disappeared one night, never to be seen again.

Now the legend goes that Thomas Moore roams the streets, maybe searching for his lost love. Whatever the reason, his phantom was seen in a bookstore on Duke of Gloucester Street in the 1980s. All of the employees except the manager had gone home. She had stayed to do the day's receipts and heard a noise from the front. She investigated and found a strange, pale man dressed all in black. Scared, she locked herself in her office and dialed 911. When she heard pounding and saw it was the police, they searched the building, but discovered no one other than her in the place.

The ghost also appeared at a jewelry store, peering in the window. He dissipated... before the worker's eyes.

I checked the shops of Henry Street and asked some employees if anyone had any encounters with the supernatural. No one did. Seems that either Thomas found his lover or maybe his wanderlust overtook him and he decided to haunt somewhere else.

A Very Haunted House

Sometimes a writer of ghost books can discover a story in the most unexpected way. When I walked over to a costumed employee in front of the Capitol in Colonial Williamsburg to ask her where a couple of buildings I was searching for were, she didn't know. I somehow ended up telling her that I was writing this book and she began to tell me of her experiences in what she called a "very haunted house" in Williamsburg.

The house is on Hickory Signpost Road. The owner never believed it was haunted... at least that was what he told her. She didn't want her name in the book, but said to go ahead and put in her story.

She lived in the basement of the house. One night she woke up and went to the living room to get a drink of water. To her shock, she saw a Civil War soldier standing right in front of the television. He was holding an arm that was hanging by a thread from his shoulder. She ran back to get her fiancée out of bed and had him come back with her to the living room. The soldier was still there and her fiancée saw him — then the spirit dissipated.

That was not the only paranormal experience she had either. She told me there were other Civil War soldiers, Revolutionary War soldiers, Indians, and even two teenage boys who crashed their car in a ravine behind the house, killing themselves. She had enough with all the spirits and moved out, but the teenage ghosts followed her to her new residence and she had to have it blessed three times before she got rid of them. She said that it made her sound like she was crazy, but the priest who blessed her home told her he saw the boys himself on the third blessing.

Some places are like magnets for the paranormal — some people can be too. In this situation, this particular person, whether she was the magnet or the house itself, was glad to be rid of all the paranormal activity.

Chapter Two

COLONIAL WILLIAMSBURG

"History is a relentless master. It has no present, only the past rushing into the future.
To try to hold fast is to be swept aside." — John F. Kennedy

Called a "living museum" because visitors can literally immerse themselves into an era of time, Colonial Williamsburg is an attraction that is both fun and educational. Visitors get to tour public buildings, homes, and trade shops of the eighteenth century, all set just before the Revolution.

Reverend Dr. W. A. R. Goodwin, the Rector of Bruton Parish Church, saw the need to preserve the historic buildings of Williamsburg and approached John D. Rockefeller, Jr. with the vision he had. Restoration began in 1926.

There are costumed actors who portray both famous and ordinary citizens of the time. Tourists are drawn into it all. They can dine in a tavern or take coffee at Carlton's Coffee House or find out what the silversmith has to offer in his shop. Politics that brought on the Revolutionary War are discussed and acted out here by actors. One can learn what tools were used, what religions were worshipped, how the African-American slaves and freeman felt, how the family lived back then, and what kinds of different foods were eaten. Holidays are celebrated here just as they were back in the eighteenth century.

Besides the taverns, shops, and homes, there are museums too. One of these museums is in a former hospital for the mentally disturbed and it has had paranormal occurrences. There are a couple of colonial houses in the Historic Area that one can stay at overnight, but beware — they are haunted. If not, then the nearby hotels may be more what you are looking for if you want a good night's sleep without uninvited supernatural guests.

Spirits of the colonists still make their home here at Colonial Williamsburg. Many accounts of paranormal activity have occurred in the 175-acre village since it first opened. There are even a few ghost tours that you can take to learn all about this other side of Colonial Williamsburg.

Just as you will find out about when you read the next few pages...for the history here is quite spirited.

Entrance to Colonial Williamsburg's Visitor Center.

One of Colonial Williamsburg's buses that takes you to the Historic Area.

Two costumed employees sitting on a bench at night.

GOVERNOR'S PALACE

When the original building was completed in 1722, it was considered one of the finest such places in America. Remember, during this time the colonies were mostly rural. Even the affluent citizens lived in one-story houses with only two or three rooms. Interior plaster walls and glass windows only existed in homes of those who could afford it, for those had to come over from England. So something like the palace was incredible.

Governor's Palace.

Alexander Spotswood became governor of the Virginia Colony in 1710. Soon after his arrival in Williamsburg, he set about improving the palace, thus raising his status as governor. Construction began in 1706, but proceeded slowly and it was no more than an enclosed shell when he first got there. He moved into the house in 1716, though it wouldn't be completed for another six years.

By 1751, the palace fell into such ruinous condition that then-Governor Robert Dinwiddie had to move into the house next door, the Robert Carter House. Extensive repairs were then done. In 1752, the governor and his family moved in, even though some repairs were still being made.

The last royal governor was John Murray, fourth Earl of Dunmore. With the American Revolution, Murray and his family fled Williamsburg. All in all, seven royal governors made the palace their residence.

During the Revolutionary War, the place was used as a hospital by the Americans. The orchard terrace overlooking the canal served as burial ground for 156 American soldiers.

After Virginia became the new commonwealth, the first two governors to live in the palace were Patrick Henry and Thomas Jefferson. Though Jefferson drew up a series of drawings for changes to the palace, they were never implemented, as the government moved to Richmond in 1780.

On December 22, 1781, the palace caught fire and burned to the ground. After the burnt skeletal remains were pulled down and the sale of the bricks, all that proved the building ever existed were its flanking advance buildings and outlying dependencies.

Years flew by and when Colonial Williamsburg started on the restoration, the palace got rebuilt, based on original blueprints. It was when archeologists rummaged through the garden to see what plants might have grown in it that they found that more than flowers had been planted in its grounds. They dug up 156 skeletons of men and two women who had been buried in the garden when the palace served as a hospital. Also with the bodies they discovered musket balls with deeply imbedded teeth marks. Unlike today when a surgeon performs surgery on a patient by delivering anesthesia, those operated on during the Revolutionary and Civil Wars had musket balls or bullets placed between their teeth to bite down on when amputations were done.

Front hall of Governor's Palace with swords on walls.

Explanations for the men were easy to figure out, but who were the women? Were they wives who had followed their husbands to war or nurses who worked in the hospital and died?

Countless ghost stories were told about the maze garden, including sightings of Red Coat Guards with muskets in hand. Another story is about a mischievous nine-year-old boy who once played on the front lawn of the Governor's Palace with a friend. After their deaths, the boys continued to be seen at night, jumping over the wall and playing with their hoops.

Some have witnessed a light going from window to window on the third floor. One security guard for Colonial Williamsburg had caught sight of the light one night. He thought it looked like a flame from a lantern. Upset, he went inside to find out who had broken in, but he found nothing. When he locked up and walked away, he happened to look back. Chills rushed over him as he saw the light again passing the windows of the top floor.

There's an urban legend told that the spirit of a criminally insane mental hospital patient haunts the wall in front of the palace. It's said that he escaped from the Eastern State Mental Institute, where he slit a woman's throat in the 1920s.

Bill and I took a tour of the palace in August 2009, when we did Colonial Williamsburg for the first time. The recorder was used, but all I got was the guide telling us about the building and its history. Interestingly enough, of the few places I visited during the daytime, I did capture an orb, at least in the hallway where the display of swords and muskets on the walls are. Was something either curious about the crowds of tourists or maybe even listening to the guide?

The Governor's Palace is at the end of the Palace Green, which runs south to north for two blocks. When you take a tour of the palace, don't be surprised if you get the sensation that something more than the living is inside it.

THE ROBERT CARTER HOUSE

No one knows who built the Robert Carter house, though it was most likely built in the 1740s. In 1751, the Virginia Colony bought the place so Governor Robert Dinwiddie had somewhere to live while the Governor's Palace was undergoing renovations. Robert Carter Nicholas took over the house in 1753. In 1761, it became Robert Carter III's property and still bears his name to this day.

An interesting characteristic of the building is its unusually long, covered veranda. Today, it connects the house with the McKenzie Apothecary.

Besides this house, Carter also owned the Nomini Plantation. When he came to live at the residence in Williamsburg, he brought his wife and eleven children. They had six more as the years passed. They had to move back to the much bigger Nomini Hall to accommodate their large family.

In the mid-nineteenth century, the Carter house was owned by Robert Saunders and his family. President of the College of William and Mary, he was also the mayor of Williamsburg for many years. A descendent of a wealthy family, Saunders owned many slaves and the entire block his house stood on. His wife was the daughter of Governor Jon Page and owned many fine and rare historical books and documents that she kept in the library in the house.

One night, as they were eating dinner, the Saunders got wind of the Union Army marching into town and fled, leaving their house unguarded. The next day after the battle, Federal soldiers ransacked the place, stealing many of its valuable treasures. They left the interior in ruins. Worse, the Saunders' neighbors came in after the soldiers left and took whatever they could find.

The Robert Carter House.

A Federal provost marshal, Major Wheeling, occupied the Robert Carter home. One night some Rebels surrounded it, and in fear, Wheeling fired his gun, not knowing if he could hit anything or not. He did — one young Rebel was hit. Abandoned by his comrades, he died.

Over the years, the ghost of this Rebel has haunted the area. Witnesses caught a glimpse of his moonlit silhouette in the night. He is always running in the ravines of the Carter House. One resident of the house from the 1960s, Alan Packwood, observed the spirit many times when he lived there. He awakened to the sound of leaves crackling and looked through the window to see a darkened figure darting from tree to tree. The figure always seemed to be carrying something long that glistened in the moonlight.

When Packwood investigated the story behind the nightly vigil, he found an article about the Confederate soldier. His body had been found with a silver saber!

On moonlit nights, if you have the chance to pass the Robert Carter house, don't be shocked if you see someone running away. It's probably just the soldier still acting out the raid and his death.

GEORGE WYTHE HOUSE

"The boundaries which divide Life from Death are at best shadowy and vague.
Who shall say where the one ends, and where the other begins?"
— Edgar Allan Poe

There is a legend told for years that Ann Skipwith haunts the George Wythe house. George Wythe was a patriot, Thomas Jefferson's teacher, and the first law professor of the United States. Ann Skipwith's legend begins when she and her husband, Sir Peyton, visited Wythe at his home.

She and her husband took up residence in Mecklenburg, Virginia, but visited the Colonial capital many times, sometimes for weeks at a time. During one of these visits they attended a gala at the Governor's Palace. The couple had an argument there when Ann thought her husband was consorting with her sister. She took off in a bad mood.

She bolted for the Wythe House, losing one of her slippers during her flight. Not stopping to find it, she rushed on through the front door of the house and bounded upstairs. The clock struck twelve at that moment. With only one shoe on, she made an odd clicking noise all the way up the stairs in that dark and empty house. The most interesting thing about this tale is if no one was inside the house at the time, how did they know she made a clicking noise, especially when years later the ghost stories started up with that sound being the focus? Some witnesses thought the sound came from someone with a peg leg.

Besides the fact that no one was home to even see how she entered or what she did, there are those who speculated that she committed suicide over her husband's infidelities. The actual truth is she died in childbirth in 1779. Peyton did marry her sister, Jean, eight to nine years after her death. Why wait that long if they were involved as supposedly they were? Another myth laid to rest is the fact that though Peyton and Ann paid extended visits to Wythe House they never lived there, so it is doubtful Ann haunts the house. Whoever does, it's not her.

George Wythe House.

Orb on desk in second floor room of Wythe House.

How the owner of the house itself, George Wythe, died has spawned a story worthy of Edgar Allan Poe himself. It is told that his grandnephew poisoned him in anticipation of a great inheritance, but Wythe lived long enough to write this nephew out of his will. Further, George did not die in Wythe House, but passed away in Richmond in 1806.

Who haunts the Wythe House? Who is behind the noises I have heard about from some workers at Colonial Williamsburg? Is it truly Lady Ann, maybe George, or someone else who haunts the place? One of the owners of the Blue Moon Antique Mall and Bookstore in Nelson County, Virginia, who used to go to college in Williamsburg and worked at Colonial Williamsburg, told me of some instances that happened in the house — disembodied voices called out names of those working there, footsteps heard on the second floor, and shadowy figures seen at night in the darkened hallways by security.

One day an employee was working alone and saw a dark outline of a man standing in the hallway he was in. This man disappeared right before his eyes!

A visitor caught sight of a woman in colonial clothing in one of the rooms, but when she looked away and then turned back, the woman wasn't there. A strong odor of antiseptic was the only evidence that the spirit had been there.

I myself caught an orb by a desk in one of the rooms, but that was it. No voices or odd noises out of context on my recorder and no other pictures.

We'll never know for sure who roams among the walls, or even how many lost souls, at least not for now. It's just another ghostly happening in Colonial Williamsburg.

PUBLIC HOSPITAL

"I became insane, with long intervals of horrible sanity." — Edgar Allan Poe

Proposal of the Public Hospital to the House of Burgesses came from Francis Fauquier, one of Virginia's royal governors. He did this in 1766. At that time the insane were cared for at home or confined with vagrants in parish workhouses. Some even became incarcerated in the Public Goal.

The General Assembly passed legislation in 1770, and the Public Hospital opened in 1773. It was the first place of its kind in British North America, only taking in the mentally unstable. Philadelphia architect Robert Smith designed the building. Trustees for it included George Wythe, Thomas Nelson, and John Blair. The hospital took care of the insane until 1885 when a fire swept through the building. It was rebuilt and used until the Eastern State Hospital on the outskirts of Williamsburg opened in the mid-1960s.

The Public Hospital.

One of the patients' cells.

The Public Hospital was the last building that Colonial Williamsburg restored. They put exhibitions of how people with mental instability were treated in America from the eighteenth to nineteenth centuries. An underground concourse connects the hospital with the two-level DeWitt Wallace Decorative Arts Museum and the Abby Rockefeller Folk Art Museum.

With its background, how can there not be ghost stories about the place? For years, those incarcerated in the hospital suffered terrible conditions. Until one doctor, Dr. John Minson Galt II, became superintendent.

Galt worked to change the patients' lives in the place. He believed that they should be treated with kindness and understanding. No one was shackled to walls. They learned to play instruments and were given clean beds to sleep on, warm blankets, and decent meals.

Then the Battle of Williamsburg happened and the Union army occupied the city. They evicted the doctor from the hospital. Patients were either locked away or set free to wander. The doctor grew depressed of how his patients were treated. One day, they found him dead from an overdose of laudanum in his home. Because of the amount he took, it caused the vessels in his brain to burst. Blood pooled on the floor beneath his head. Not long after, the Lee family moved in. Mrs. Lee said no matter how much she scrubbed the floor she couldn't get the bloodstain out of the floorboards. They took out that floor and replaced it. The next morning they found that floorboard stained with blood! Even more frightening was the man her children saw upstairs in the room where the doctor died.

When the Lees moved, the house got torn down and no one has claimed seeing anything in that area anymore...but there are hauntings in the hospital. In the mornings, the bed in the exhibition room appears to have been slept in — even though no one is in the building at night. Tourists complain of gusts of wind in the halls. There is even the feeling of being watched by something unseen. Items in the hospital would disappear one day and reappear the next day.

Who haunts the hall and rooms of the hospital? Is it the doctor, or maybe even the patients who stayed there? I can't tell you. I got one faint voice in a recording, but I couldn't tell what it said. I also had a strange feeling at one end of the hall, but nothing unusual appeared in any of my photos.

When you take a tour of the Public Hospital and a strange gust of wind sweeps past you, don't be alarmed — it may be just the doctor rushing to a patient. After all, you can't keep a good doctor dead.

THE COKE-BARRETT HOUSE

Located near the intersection of Waller Road and Nicholson Street is the Coke-Barrett house. It seems quiet when you pass it. Well, quiet, except for the ghost of the Confederate.

The Coke-Barrett house was put to use as a makeshift hospital when the Civil War raged in Williamsburg. Dr. Barrett was a surgeon and he worked on many of the casualties brought in from the Battle of Williamsburg, not caring what side the wounded were on. Amputations of both arms and legs had to be done many times, and these piled up in all corners of his surgical office.

The dead were wrapped in sheets and buried in mass graves. Amputation pits were dug to bury the parts taken from the bodies. Like many places used as hospitals during the Civil War, this place became haunted.

A Confederate had fallen to save a comrade. Shot by a Union cavalryman as he hoisted his friend up on his shoulder to carry him, he dragged himself and his fellow soldier to the Coke-Garrett house. His friend survived. He did not. Now, his spirit has been seen on the grounds. He is dressed in the gray uniform of the Rebels and there is a bloody mark on his chest where he had been hit.

One witness, Mary, has seen him on a number of occasions. He is always on the ground, moaning in pain. Others have seen him too. A tourist said she was visiting Colonial Williamsburg and had just passed the jail when she saw the man on the ground, obviously in pain. She ran to help him and glanced over her shoulder to call to a friend to help, but when she looked back, the man was gone. Both she and the friend searched, but never found him.

Terrible tragedy strikes and someone dies — leaving us with haunted reasons on why war is so horrible.

The Coke-Barrett House.

THE LUDWELL-PARADISE HOUSE

Lying halfway between Queen and Colonial Streets on Duke of Gloucester Street, the Ludwell-Paradise House is next to the Prentis Store.

Although there had been an earlier structure on the site, the dwelling seen today was built by Philip Ludwell, III around 1755. Ludwell's daughter, Lucy Ludwell-Paradise, lived in the place in the 1800s. A press was operated by William Rind and then his widow, Clementina, on the property. This was the first property that John D. Rockefeller Jr. purchased in Williamsburg, for only $8,000. The house opened as an exhibition in April 1935, four months after it had been restored. The building exhibited Abby Aldrich Rockefeller's folk art collection at one time.

Lucy inherited the house when Philip Ludwell III passed away. Considered not nice or kind, Lucy was never popular with the townspeople. She married John Paradise and the couple lived in London, so Lucy rented out the house in Williamsburg. After the Revolution, Lucy nearly lost her home when the new Commonwealth tried to confiscate it. When John died, Lucy found herself penniless and alone, so she returned to Williamsburg, though it didn't happen until 1805, as she had to get permission to return and had to fight to get her home back.

The Ludwell-Paradise House.

Lucy had grown eccentric over the years she had been away from Williamsburg. So eccentric that it bordered on lunacy. She thought of herself as royalty. She would parade up and down Duke of Gloucester Street and wave like a queen, as her servant walked behind her, holding her skirt as if Lucy were a bride marching down the aisle. Not long after this, she snuck into her neighbors' homes to steal clothing. She'd dress in several dresses and hats before strutting down the street like a queen.

When she coerced neighbors to take make-believe carriage rides with her in her stable, the townspeople had her committed to the Public Hospital in 1816. Fighting all the way, five men had to carry her to the hospital. Two years after her incarceration, insane Lucy died in the asylum.

There was no word of hauntings until the restoration began. This is when things like the paranormal usually do occur. Workers complained of odd things. One of the workers left a letter that told of tools going missing and papers scattered about. Documents needed to renovate the place could not be found. Pounding noises came from rooms no one was in and water was being turned on and off.

Does Lucy still haunt the house today? During stops at the house on ghost tours, some tourists have claimed to see Lucy Ludwell's ghost waving from a window.

If you chance to go pass the house late one evening when the streets are almost empty and look up at it, don't be surprised if you see a woman at one of the windows, giving you a queenly wave. It's only Lucy.

CHOWNING'S TAVERN

When Josiah Chowning opened his tavern in 1766, he wanted to appeal to the ordinary people and, when Colonial Williamsburg reconstructed this tavern in the 1940s, they assumed they were doing so on the *right* original foundation, but they weren't. Instead the foundation belonged to a privately owned home — a fact I learned when I took the Colonial Williamsburg Tavern Ghost Walk.

Located on Duke of Gloucester Street next to Market Square and the Courthouse, the tavern allows casual attire and no reservations are necessary. Instead, seating is based on space availability. There are ales and specialty alcoholic drinks that you can order besides fountain drinks and water; the menu features sandwiches, light fare, stews, and desserts.

However, people don't just come for a bite to eat or to squelch their thirst. Indeed, there are more than sandwiches at this tavern — there are specters haunting within these walls. Things of an unusual nature commonly take place at Chowning's Tavern: furniture moving around, clothing of tourists being yanked on, and a little girl who appears and disappears.

Bill and I arrived early for the ghost tour to start, so we stopped at Chowning's for root beer. Seated by the window, we watched a magician who came into the dining room to perform. I took a couple of photos of him. In one of them, I discovered what looked like an orb starting to form behind his head. Is this the ghost that uses the tavern for his stomping grounds?

Seven years ago, a woman was eating when the server approached her table, asking if she needed anything more. The woman looked at him and said, "I'm psychic. Did you know this tavern was haunted?" She gestured to the side. "Seems Peter told me he's the one haunting it and he is very, very fond of a hostess named Emily that you have working here."

Orbs and possibly more at Chowning's Tavern during the Tavern Ghost Walk

When Lee, the server, admitted they had an Emily who worked as a hostess there, he went to get her, as the psychic directed. The woman stood with him at the table, not sure what was going on.

The psychic looked up at Emily. She told her that a spirit named Peter who haunted the place liked her. That he felt he was the protector of her and her newborn son who came too soon.

This did bother Emily that the woman knew about her son who had been born a preemie. She glanced aside at Lee, but Lee told her he never said a thing to the woman.

"I don't know how you knew about my baby, but I don't believe in ghosts," Emily said. "I am not buying the Peter story."

The woman smiled and said that was too bad, as Peter really liked her. He even brought her a white flower yesterday.

Emily turned white as the flower. When she had been seating some people in the gardens, she found a white magnolia blossom at her feet that hadn't been there earlier. The thing about this is the nearest magnolia bush was two blocks away, by the Peyton Randolph house. No way for it to come from any flowering bush nearby — at least not on its own. The day after meeting the psychic, Emily quit.

It goes to show that a woman can have a male stalker — even if he is the ghost of a man from the eighteenth century!

The next time you need someplace to sit and relax, why not have a drink at Chowning's. Let it be known, though, that if you find a white flower at your feet…you may be the object of some phantom's affections!

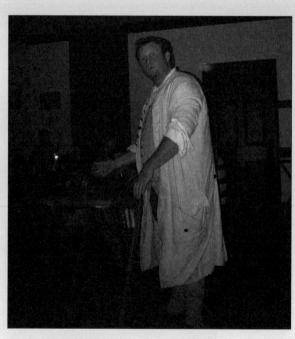

Could an orb be forming behind the head of this performing magician?

SHIELDS TAVERN

Shields Tavern is a place in Colonial Williamsburg where you can stop for a bite to eat in an eighteenth century setting after a day of walking through the Historic Area. It is on Duke of Gloucester Street near the Capitol. Reservations are required.

Unlike Shields and other taverns in the Historic Area, in the eighteenth century taverns provided comfortable lodgings for travelers, as well as being places to gather for meals, conversation, and entertainment. Proprietors prided themselves on serving filling meals using the freshest ingredients.

Ghost Walk

On August 15, 2009, Bill and I took the 7 p.m. Colonial Williamsburg Tavern Ghost Walk. We saw a growing crowd of people — men, women, teenagers, and children — milling around Shields Tavern. A story bandied about is there's a woman in a green dress that has been seen by several different employees. We checked in and went to stand for a while until the tour started. I took a few pictures while we did, and we talked to some of the people, too. Our guide that night was Lindsey; we gathered around her and the crowd hushed, as she gave out some basic rules and launched into the first story about Shields.

Shields Tavern during the daytime.

When Colonial Williamsburg wanted to keep the streets (such as Duke of Gloucester in front of Shields) like they were in the eighteenth century, with just human foot traffic and horses and buggies, they built a tunnel underground that led from Francis Street to where Shields and Kings Arms are. It also led to a very big kitchen beneath ground where they could cook and bring food up by staircase to those eating in the taverns above.

One night seven years ago, after everything was closed up, one assistant manager, Denise, was making sure all of the candles were out and the lights were off. Then she went downstairs to the kitchen and from there through the tunnel until she was outside. She happened to glance back and saw a light on in an upstairs room in the tavern, so she stomped back through the tunnel to the kitchen and upstairs to the room where the light was on. She hit the light switch and shut off the light.

She went back downstairs and ended up outside, where a dishwasher was waiting for his ride. When she looked back at Shields, the light was on again!

Turning to the dishwasher, she said, "Look at the building for me. Tell me what you see."

He turned and said, "Oh, my Lord!"

"You're going with me." She dragged him back with her through the tunnel, to the kitchen, and upstairs.

Well, the dishwasher refused to go upstairs to the room where the light came from, so Denise tromped up the steps to the room and stuck her head in. To her shock, she found not only the light on, but also the entire room in total disarray. All of the furniture has been rearranged.

Shields Tavern at night before the Tavern Ghost Walk.

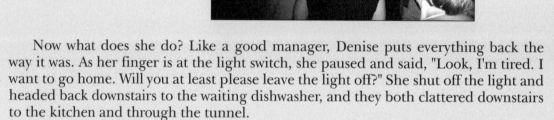

There's an orb above the tour guide's head as she tells ghost stories about Shields Tavern.

Now what does she do? Like a good manager, Denise puts everything back the way it was. As her finger is at the light switch, she paused and said, "Look, I'm tired. I want to go home. Will you at least please leave the light off?" She shut off the light and headed back downstairs to the waiting dishwasher, and they both clattered downstairs to the kitchen and through the tunnel.

Once outside both of them turned around to glance back at the tavern to the window of the room that had the light on twice. The light wasn't on, but they saw the silhouette of a man in a tricorn hat watching them from the rear center window!

No, they did not go back there that night.

Before Shields, there had been a tavern called Monroe's Ordinary there for two decades in the eighteenth century, but Mr. Monroe met an untimely death. His best friend, Mr. Sharp, was arrested for his murder. Five of the most prominent men spoke against him, saying he had killed Mr. Monroe, but Sharp was acquitted and he went on to open a tavern right across from where Monroe had his.

Two ghost walk guides were talking about the murder when one of them, Kelly, asked the other, Jenny, if she felt cold.

"Yes, on my left side," Jenny replied.

"I feel it on my right side," Kelly said.

That's when they realized that an icy unseen presence stood between them. Was Monroe listening to them?

Another time, Jenny was closing up the tavern and walked upstairs to her office. As she sat at her desk, she heard the sound of footsteps stomping down below and up the stairs to her room. She wondered if an angry guest had gotten locked in by mistake or left behind from a ghost walk. When she looked through the window, though, she saw Kelly leading her tour group — and Jenny realized that she was completely alone in the building.

One time, Kelly discovered she had two psychics in her group. As she talked about Monroe, they broke in, telling her that a man in eighteenth century clothing was leaning at the window and seemed to be listening to her.

They went on to tell her that he had a special interest in her and liked to play tricks on her, too. Like locking and unlocking doors on her. That made sense to her as six months before she had gone upstairs to use the handicapped bathroom and had locked it behind her. A tiny bit later, she heard a click, like the door had unlocked. She washed her hands and walked over to the door, finding it had been unlocked.

A woman who ate in the tavern saw a man in eighteenth century clothing walking around and looking over the tables. She realized he had to be a ghost when no one else appeared to acknowledge he was there. He looked at her as if he knew she could see him and then walked through the doorway.

Someone else saw him standing on the steps one day. He looked away and then back at the spot... The man had vanished. No one was there. When he glanced at a mirror nearby, he saw the man standing on the steps.

A young woman who claimed to be a paranormal investigator asked if she could do an EVP session with her digital recorder. She asked several questions. Then she switched it on to listen to and heard only one answer, to her last question. She had asked, "Do you want me to leave?"

A voice answered, "Go away."

Some years ago, in the winter, the ghost tour was moved inside Shields because it was supposed to be cold. They set up a place in the entrance room called the hall. There's another room called the lower room that can only be reached by going through the hall. There were two tours like usual, one at 7 p.m. and one at 9 p.m. People came into the hall that had a fire going, sat down, and listened to the ghost stories in there. After each presentation, the guide would open up the door to the lower room because they could tell some more tales about people seeing things in the mirror in the room.

Some people who went to eat elsewhere before the 9 p.m. presentation as Shields was closed that day. When they came back close to 9, they told the guide that they had seen a man and a woman sitting at the table, right by that window with the candle lit, and it looked like they were eating dinner. That was why the couple had asked the guide the first time around if they could eat dinner in the tavern; they thought it was open.

After the Ghost Tour

Bill and I got to be inside Shields after it was closed. Led by another guide named Tim McCarthy, not only were we were told more ghost stories about the place, but I also got to do a little paranormal investigating of my own to see if I could catch anything by photograph or EVP. I caught something faint on my recorder as I walked downstairs to the basement dining room. I couldn't tell if it were footsteps or something else.

Next time you eat at Shields and you see a gentleman dressed in eighteenth century clothing staring at you, don't worry. It's just their ghost making sure your meal has that added supernatural flair.

Inside Shields at night after the Tavern Ghost Walk.

The underground kitchen beneath Shields Tavern.

The underground tunnel beneath Colonial Williamsburg that ends at Francis Street.

PARTY ON AT RALEIGH TAVERN

If you feel the need to get a bite to eat, but don't want to eat inside if it's a nice day, then Raleigh Tavern has a bakery behind it. There are ham biscuits, Sally Lunn bread, rolls, queen's cake, ginger ale, cider, root beer, and even mouth-watering gingerbread can be gotten there. Then you can find a spot somewhere in the backyard of the tavern and enjoy a quick lunch in pleasant surroundings. Built around 1717, the tavern was popular. Many came, including important people of the day. Local gossip and current events set the scene here.

Besides good food and drink, gambling seemed to be another pastime here. When the ground was excavated here, dice boxes were found. One man who also was a butcher, John Custis, had lost heavily at gambling and was discovered dead, his throat cut. Important decisions about the Patriots' revolt against the British took place here, and many balls were also held here. In the Apollo Room, George Washington received a surprise birthday party. Night after night, gala parties happened, with the last one to do with Marquis de Lafayette. Not long after that, in December 1859, fire raged through the tavern and it burned to the ground. When Colonial Williamsburg began restoration of the Historic Area, the tavern was rebuilt on the foundations of the original one.

Three years before the fire and after the place had closed for the night, one man wrote a letter to a friend, talking about something strange that had happened to him. Samuel Armistead was walking his dog one evening in January. When he drew close to the tavern, he heard laughter and sounds of merriment going on in the building. He knew that the place had been quiet for years and it was dark that night. A hint of tobacco wafted to his nose. Curious, he peeked through a window and found it empty of life!

Modern times were no exception to the ghostly goings-on of the tavern. A custodian for Colonial Williamsburg heard laughter and music himself one night as he was cleaning up in back of the building. He drew closer and smelled pipe tobacco. All of the noises ended when he peeked inside.

If you chance to walk past Raleigh's Tavern when it is already dark and happen to spy a light coming from its windows and hear laughter, just keep on going. The only parties being held there are for the dead, not the living.

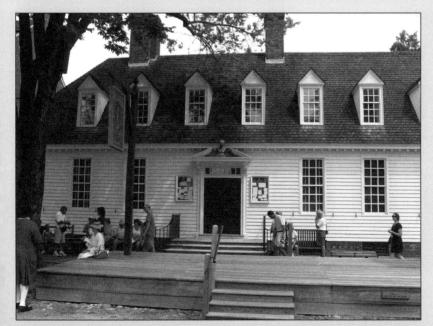

Raleigh Tavern.

FORCED TO MOVE

Dora Armistead's house was moved from where it had been on Duke of Gloucester Street to where it now sits at North Henry Street. Colonial Williamsburg was behind the move, since the house did not fit into the Colonial era. This did not sit well with Doris, whose spirit followed the house to its new location and now haunts the place.

William Armistead came to the New World in 1635, and acquired land in Virginia by 1651. Unfortunately, when the Civil War came around, the family lost both their land and money when the Union Army confiscated it.

Now homeless, Cary Peyton Armistead rose above it and got enough money saved to buy a house on Duke of Gloucester Street, but termites infested the place and he tore it down, building a twelve-room Victorian house, which he occupied with his wife, Endora, and their five children.

Cary passed away in 1901, leaving his family destitute. Endora took a job at the Public Hospital. The eldest of the five children died. She made enough money to put the others through college. The two men became lawyers and the two women, teachers. They all lived at the house.

When Colonial Williamsburg started to take over and restored much of the area, Endora refused to sell the house. After she and her two sons died, the two sisters, Dora and Cara, remained in the house. To make money, they turned the house into an inn. Cara loved it, as the tourism made money, but Dora preferred peace and quiet and did not care for all the tourists.

Armistead House.

Cara passed away in 1979. Dora followed her in 1984 at the age of ninety-three. The Association for Preservation for Virginia turned the house into a museum, but later it became unoccupied — at least by the living. Occasionally, someone would see curtains being moved at the window of what had been Dora's bedroom and, in 1995, when Colonial Williamsburg moved the house to its present location, that sight of curtains moving grew worse. A crowd gathered around the building, watching the curtains blowing at a furious pace. All of the windows and doors were closed and there was no electricity. There was no reason for any air to be other than still within the walls. Besides the curtains, people have complained feeling as if someone was glaring at them as they passed the house.

I took a picture of the house when we visited Colonial Williamsburg. I admit I didn't feel anything, nor did I see the curtains move. Maybe by the time I had found the house, Dora had given up and had joined her family in the afterlife.

However, if I am wrong, be careful when you walk pass the house. If you see a part of the curtain at a second-story window shift and feel someone is staring at you, just keep on going and don't stop. It's only Dora wanting peace and quiet.

You can find the house about a block from Merchants Square, near the corner of North Henry and Scotland Streets. The building is not open to the public.

THE PALMER HOUSE

"His body was transparent; so that Scrooge, observing him, and looking through his waistcoat, could see the two buttons on his coat behind." — Charles Dickens

The building was built by Alexander Kerr in the 1730s, but it was in the 1740s that John Palmer and his family moved into the house. John was a lawyer and bursar for the College of William and Mary.

In 1754, the Palmers awoke to a fire ablaze in their home. It burned the place down and Mr. Palmer replaced it with the structure that still stands on the property today. He modeled it after a London townhouse favored by London society. It is taller than other eighteenth century Williamsburg homes as it stood on a hill and had a higher roof. The holes in the house's outer walls were made by brick masons to secure scaffolding, and left unplugged, so that any time the place needed a repair, it could be done.

By the 1860s, a local merchant, William Vest, owned it. The richest man in town, Vest expanded the place, by building a duplicate on the back section. That section was torn down to return the house to its original eighteenth century look when Colonial Williamsburg began its restoration. Worried by the Civil War, Vest took his family and fled to Richmond. It would be several years before they returned home.

The house became headquarters for Confederate Generals Joseph Johnston and James Longstreet, but on May 4, 1862, when they learned that the Northern troops were heading toward Williamsburg, they fled with their troops to Richmond. When the Federals marched into town, General George McClellan took the house over. A week later, he joined his troops to pursue the fleeing Southern army, as he had been criticized for staying in the house instead of giving chase. Sometime after that, the Union troops descended on Williamsburg and killed off many of the men and boys. Those not killed were imprisoned, wounded, or chased out of town. All that remained were the women, children, sick, and elderly. The women wore black to show their disapproval of the Northerners.

The Palmer House was occupied by numerous Federal provost marshals during this time. One of them, David Campbell, showed neither compassion nor mercy to any of the people. Then on September 9, 1862, he was rudely awakened in the early morning hours by Confederate raiders at gunpoint and taken to Libby Prison in Richmond. Another one, Lieutenant Disosway, was the opposite of Campbell. He was kind to the people. He tried to keep any of the Northern troops from harming anyone; the women thought him of as a true Southern gentleman.

One evening he got wind of drunken soldiers harassing some women, and rushed from the Palmer House to where the soldiers were camped at Market Square. He ordered them to stay in their tents and reprimanded them. One of the soldiers grew angry and shot him. Townspeople took him to the Palmer House and waited for a doctor. Dr. Robert Major Garrett came, but could do nothing to save Disosway. He perished two hours after being shot.

Not long after, the Civil War ended and life returned somewhat back to normal for the citizens. The Northern troops withdrew, but one Northerner did not.

The Palmer House.

The Tucker family moved into the Palmer House in the 1890s. Mrs. Tucker kept a journal and made an entry dated June 23, 1896 about a ghost. The family had become aware of an unseen presence in the house. When she got up from bed to get a drink of water, she walked into the parlor and saw a man in a chair, smoking a pipe and reading a book. She noted he wore dark clothing with gold trim. Mrs. Tucker fainted. The next morning, she visited her neighbor to tell of her strange experience. Her neighbor told her she should research the house's past and see who it could be.

Mrs. Tucker found a picture and story while digging in the College of William and Mary's archives. To her shock, the picture was of the very man that had been in her parlor! His name had been Disosway. Frightened, she hoped the phantom would leave the family alone.

By 1897, Mrs. Tucker had a change of heart about the ghost she wanted out of her home. She said he was gentle and always smiled at them. Though he haunted the house for a long time, there have been no reports in recent years. Maybe Disosway thought it was time to move on.

From Secretary's Office to the House

The Capitol building burned in 1747. Many records and papers burned with it, but there were some that were not destroyed. That was when the decision to keep important documents separate from the Capitol was made and the Public Records office was built. It was also the office of the Secretary.

It was completed by December 1748, at a cost of nearly four hundred pounds. Designed to avoid fire, the building had neither a basement nor attic. Its floor was paved with stones while the interior walls and window jambs were plastered-over brick. Very little wood was used. It did have four fireplaces to provide heat in the winter and keep damp and mold away in the summer.

After the capitol and the records were moved to Richmond, the place was occupied by the Court of Admiralty under Justice Benjamin Waller. By 1855, the capitol became a school and it became the headmaster's home.

In 1862, some Confederates hid within its walls. Union troops surrounded it and kept firing until they felt the Rebels had run out of ammunition. Then they bust through the door and captured the soldiers inside.

Despite the precautions they took when they built it, a mob of runaway slaves broke down the wooden doors and set fire to the building. They wanted to destroy all records of their ownership, but the building remained standing.

Around the twentieth century, it became a home for a family: David Roland Jones, his wife, and seven daughters. None of the daughters ever married or left home. These girls would spend their days on the front lawn with their cats and nothing more. It was thought that David being religious kept a strict hold on them.

However, one of the girls, Edna, felt unhappy about her situation. Too timid to say anything, she also feared his anger. Soon, though, she had something to bring a ray of sunshine into her life. John Mince made weekly trips to the household, bringing food and supplies. Edna found herself looking forward to his visits. She began to fall in love with him and unknown to her, he with her.

John finally let known his feelings to her. She was ecstatic, but soon realized that her father would not allow this relationship to happen. She agreed to meet John at the grounds where the Governor's Palace had stood before it burned down.

Edna dressed carefully and put her red hair up. Then she slipped out, but, panicked about her father catching her, she never saw the oncoming carriage. When she did, it was too late — it ran over her.

Since that terrible night, Edna has been seen roaming the grounds, only to vanish a few seconds later. Her phantom has also been seen hovering over the Jones family cemetery, fading in and out. She has even been captured on film in the cemetery. She has been heard too.

Secretary's Office.

In 1969, Agnus Taylor noted seeing her in her diary. Agnus had been scrubbing the windows when she saw a woman in white hanging in mid-air over the old cemetery. Suddenly, she vanished!

On a tour, a psychic mentioned seeing the ghost by the building, dressed in white and with her red hair put up. She also mentioned about something wrong with her eyes. The guide found out that indeed the girl had worn glasses.

Had she had not been wearing her glasses the night she had gone to met her lover? It would be hard for a woman to let herself be seen in glasses by her beau. Maybe Edna never saw the carriage coming.

A love story gone wrong has all the makings for a haunting, as this ghost is still trying to sneak back into the house.

BASSETT HALL

"Love looks not with the eyes, but with the mind." — William Shakespeare

Bassett Hall is a two-story, eighteenth century frame house that John D. Rockefeller Jr. and his wife Abby Aldrich Rockefeller made their home in October 1927, though it would be several years before they took up residence there. It looks much like when the Rockefellers lived there during their seasonal visits. Its garden still blooms in the spring and fall, just as it did back then. Extensive, recently completed conservation work added more than 5,000 trees, shrubs, and ground cover to the garden. The trails that the Rockefellers established in the woods behind the home are still there. Mrs. Rockefeller was noted telling a local resident that her husband told her she could keep the place if she promised not to bring in tourists.

Bassett Hall was owned by the Brays from the early seventeenth century until 1753. At that point Elizabeth Bray's husband, Colonel Phillip Johnson, got it. No doubt he built the house that stands today after the property became his. There were 950 acres of land and four contiguous lots in the city of Williamsburg.

Next to own the property was Richard Corbin, who refurbished the house around 1790s. Then Burwell Bassett acquired it, and it has carried his name since. Besides being a Virginia legislator, Bassett was also the nephew of Martha Washington. Later owners of the place include President John Tyler, John Coke, Colonel Goodrich Durfey, and Israel Smith...all leading up to Rockefeller, of course.

There was a fire in 1930 that destroyed the roof and stair hall. This delayed the Rockefellers' restoration of the house. Colonial Williamsburg's landscape architect, Arthur Shurcliff, created the garden plan. The Rockefellers were interested in the arts and furnished folk art, Chinese porcelain, Oriental carpets, and European porcelain in the building.

When Abby Rockefeller passed away in 1948, her husband deeded Bassett Hall to their son, John D. Rockefeller 3rd. At his father's demise in 1960, John and his wife, Blanchette, took over the property, but a year after John 3rd's death in 1978, the family gave it to the Colonial Williamsburg Foundation. Today, tourists can visit it when they come to Colonial Williamsburg — it's all part of the ticket they purchase for the Historic Area.

Is it one of the Rockefellers that haunts the place, or even Bassett himself? No, the ghost story begins with the Durfeys, their daughter, Margaret, in particular. During the Battle of Williamsburg, a young Confederate soldier, John Lea, was wounded. He was brought to Bassett Hall, where it fell to Margaret to tend him. They fell in love with each other and wished to marry.

Now, Captain George Armstrong Custer had known John when both were classmates at West Point, even though one joined the Union Army and the other, with the Rebels. Custer also fought in the Battle of Williamsburg, and when he got wind of his friend's injuries, he rushed to John's side. When the young man was well enough, Margaret and he were married on May 23, 1862, with Custer standing by his side as his best man.

The wedding was beautiful and the party after, a splendid time for all. Custer remained a guest of the enemy until he got called back to duty. There is an inscription on a window on the ground floor of Bassett Hall to commemorate the wedding.

Besides the inscription, there seems to be a paranormal commemoration of the event, too. An employee of Colonial Williamsburg mentioned how one spring evening he heard music and laughter. All the tourists were gone for the day, and Tom was a custodian for the place, cleaning up. The voices appeared to be coming from the front. Thinking a party was going on and not wanting to intrude, he kept at his work until it was time to go. He walked around to the front expecting a party, but found not a soul!

Another worker was upstairs in the building when he spied women in long gowns and hair up and men in uniforms on the front lawn. Couples danced and others held drinks in their hands. One of the women wore what looked to him like an old-fashioned wedding gown. She danced with a handsome young man. He ran downstairs and out the front door to see, but everyone had vanished!

Sounding much like a residual haunting, it seems that a happy event can be the cause of a good haunting such as this. Maybe it's the couple reliving their wedding over and over as the result of their love for each other.

Bassett Hall is located near the Capitol, on the south side of Francis Street at the end of a long, tree-lined approach.

THE HAUNTED GAOL AND HANGMAN'S ROAD

"There are mysteries which men can only guess at, which age by age they may solve only in part." — Bram Stoker

During the 1700s the Public Gaol had evolved into a walled, three-structure compound that numbered among its inmates not only assorted miscreants, but also the keeper and his family. It is one of the oldest buildings in the city; Williamsburg began its restoration of it in 1927. The first gaoler, John Redwood, had charge of prisoners dispatched from county gaols to Williamsburg for General Court trial of cases punishable by hanging or maiming. In 1711, the General Assembly authorized a debtors' prison addition. In 1722, a keeper's house was built.

Apart from ordinary murderers, thieves, and counterfeiters, also contained within the gaol's walls were disobedient Indians; slave-revolt conspirators; pirates, which included some of Blackbeard's; and redcoat Revolutionary War trophy Henry 'Hair Buyer' Hamilton. A historical report claimed that during the Civil War, Federal troops demolished all but the original structure for bricks to build quarters. What remained served the local needs until 1910.

Some tourists leaving one of the four prison cells at the Public Gaol.

The Public Gaol.

Prisoners slept on flea-ridden straw. Lice, roaches, and rats infested the walls. It was a foul place to be incarcerated in, and many were hanged not far from the building. Some of those hanged in 1718 were fifteen of Blackbeard's crew. When they captured Blackbeard, his whole ship was arrested, too. They were hanged by the neck to give warnings to all who dare a life of piracy.

The wheels of the wagon of death would be heard creaking up Nicolson Street to take them to the gallows. Those who rode it sat on their own coffins for the mile-long ride. People gathered around the gallows for the hanging events, as this was entertainment for those days.

There's no remains left of the gallows, but the Public Gaol still stands for tourists to visit on their Colonial Williamsburg pass. One worker claimed that when she was alone, she heard laughter and banging on the walls, and people who live on Nicholson Street say that they have heard the creaking of the wheels and horses clip-clopping on the street in the predawn hours.

James Daughtery, a guest at the Coke-Barrett house in 1985, told how he awoke to wagon wheels and a cracking of a whip. Colonial Williamsburg does have its horse-drawn wagons out that early. He even heard a voice urging the horses on. He got out of bed to stand at the window. He remembered the story, but saw nothing on the street.

In 1992, a Colonial Williamsburg employee was setting up the tool display in the Carpenter's Yard when he heard the wheels and horses. He rushed out when he heard the crack of the whip, as he loved animals and wanted to catch who was mistreating the horses. Nothing was there.

Tourists who have stayed on Capitol Landing Road (this was Hangman's Road) claimed to have heard the horse and wagon too, and one woman said she was awoken by people cheering and a horse whinnying. It was pretty early and she stalked to the window angry, but found the yard empty of life.

The Author's Visit

I finally got to check out the inside of the gaol on May 19, 2010. A guide told us about the house, which was from the 1930s and had been lived in by the jailer and his family. She pointed out two branding irons on top of the mantle of the fireplace, telling me to pick one up. One of them had an "M" at the end, signifying murderer. The other had a "T," which meant the person branded was a thief.

Odd anomalies appear in the cell of the Public Gaol.

After that, the guide told us to go to the gaol's cells. All four were from the 1700s. I took some pictures both inside and outside the cells. I also recorded with my digital recorder in a couple of them. In one photo, I captured two anomalies in a cell; one looks like a light in a shape of a diamond over what must have been where food was slid to the prisoners. The other looked like half of a large blue orb up toward the ceiling. The cells were all dark and this one had a window, but the sunlight did not focus on the wall of the diamond shape at all. Are they because of my camera or are they something paranormal, I can't tell you.

The Public Gaol stands next door to the Coke-Barrett House on the eastern end of Nicholson Street. You can tour the place on a Colonial Williamsburg pass during the daytime, but not at the predawn hours to catch the wagon!

THE PEYTON RANDOLPH HOUSE

"There are more things in heaven and earth, Horatio
Than are dreamt of in your philosophy." — William Shakespeare

The building that is considered to be the most haunted is the Peyton Randolph house. It was even the basis for a student documentary by student Liz Budrionis, "The Peyton Randolph House: History and Legends," during the summer of 2006.

For research for the film, Budrionis spent several hours in the house after dark, and experienced at least one strange occurrence. One night, Budrionis and a friend knocked on the Peyton Randolph House's front door three times. She said there was a brief silence. As she turned to leave, she heard three very distinct raps on the bottom half of the door. Her friend and she bolted. Funny thing… no one, including security guards, was in the house at the time.

It is said that the Peyton Randolph House is home to as many as twenty-three ghosts.

Sir John Randolph had the home built in 1715 by William Robertson. He left the house to his wife, Susannah Beverley Randolph, until their second son, Peyton, reached the age of 24 and inherited it. The house remained in the family until 1824. That's when Mary Monroe Peachy bought it. One of her children was killed in an accident; others died of diseases. A family member even committed suicide. A boarder died from tuberculosis.

Colonial Williamsburg's primary restoration of the home began in October 1938 and was completed in April 1940. More restoration of the main section was undertaken in June 1967 and was finished twelve months later. The center and west portions of the house opened for exhibition July 1, 1968. It is located at the corner of Nicholson and North England Streets. Notable guests at the home were Rochambeau, Lafayette, and Washington.

There are several accounts of phenomena at the Peyton Randolph House, including the shattering of a mirror and the sound of heavy footsteps. The first haunting is that of a young soldier who stayed in the structure when the Peachy family owned it. At the time of his stay, he attended college to advance in his studies. Unfortunately, he fell ill. When this occurred, he was cared for the best that he could be, but he eventually died because of the devastating illness. Today, several accounts attest to the fact that the spirit of the young man still lingers in the structure. Many have stated that they have seen the apparition of a male, while others have said they have heard footsteps that seem to be quite heavy. Another ghost seen is an older woman who is dressed in a white, flowing gown. Then, there is a little girl who was thrown down the stairs and killed after her ghostly best friend, Elizabeth, grew angry with her. Doctors claimed that superhuman force would have been required to cause such a death. Another ghost supposedly hangs around in the upstairs bedroom.

Another story is told of a ghost of a woman who seemed very agitated and wanted to warn guests of impending danger. A woman named Helen Hall Mason stayed for a friend's wedding at the house in 1962. She stayed as a guest of its owner at the time in the oak-paneled room, which was on the second floor toward the back of the house. Sometime during the night, Mrs. Mason woke up and saw a woman standing at the foot of the bed, appearing very nervous and wringing her hands. At first, Mrs. Mason thought that it was the hostess of the house…until she noticed that the woman's dress wasn't modern. A scarier thing — moonbeams went right through the woman. Mrs. Mason mentioned what happened the next morning. She didn't feel threatened by this woman, but felt that the woman was trying to give a message of warning to her. The hosts said that Mrs. Mason's story matched that of other stories over the years. Not much is known about this ghost, except that she might be a servant.

Peyton Randolph House.

Other tales of hauntings permeate this place. One of them concerned a two-year-old girl who was sleeping in an upstairs bedroom. She woke up, screaming for her mother. The child mumbled about a man in white standing in a corner, but the mother saw no one there. Some years later, a man sleeping in the same bedchamber saw a transparent male form standing in a corner.

Another story tells of Williamsburg employees who saw a man in blue Colonial attire. Thinking he was one of them, they went to talk to him. He vanished when they approached.

An interpreter was alone in the house when she felt something trying to push her down the stairs. It terrified her as she felt it was evil. There was also the tale about what happened to security guard Pedro Jones. He was getting ready to leave when he heard groans emanating from the basement. He went down to investigate. The door slammed shut on him, locking him in. He couldn't get out and suffered being down there until his boss knocked on the door. That's when the door mysteriously unlocked and Jones was able to get out.

Ghost Walk

On the Colonial Williamsburg Tavern Ghost Walk, I learned of some more occurrences that happened to the workers and tourists inside the house.

Lindsay had led us to the house and stood on the porch before the front door. We surrounded her in a half-moon arc. Bill and I were on the left side of the house if you faced it from the street. It was dark, adding an eerie ambiance to the building.

I snapped pictures of Lindsay on the stoop, the crowd, and the house. Meanwhile, Lindsay began telling us some stories.

Orbs at Peyton Randolph House at night.

One of these concerned a security guard. Every night, after the buildings closed, security sends out their guards to check the places over and to make sure everything is all right. The guard had been going through the building and just walked into the basement, his flashlight lighting his way.

Well, back at Dispatch, they hadn't heard from him in a while and sent a squad car to the Randolph house to see what happened. They searched the place and saw a light flickering off and on. They followed it down to the basement and found their man. He crouched down on the floor, his left hand holding the flashlight over his shoulder and his gun out of his holster and held in the other, cocked. He looked terrified. Lucky for them, he did not shoot them. The supervisor contacted him and asked what happened to him down in the basement to freak him out so.

He simply said, "I quit — and I will never step on Colonial Williamsburg property ever again."

No one has ever heard what did happen to him.

Some other security guards one time saw five men having an argument on the staircase. The guards drew closer and closer, and the men never acknowledged them at all. Then when one of the guards hit the banister, the men vanished.

One of the ghost tour guides, Jenny, never stands on the stoop anymore. She used to when she told stories of the house to her groups, but some time ago, she heard a knocking from inside the house, on the front door. She told her group that it was Security playing a joke on her, so she called Security about it. The man on-duty answered. He told her that he did some checking and that no one was in the house when she brought her group by. Another incident that put the capper on her standing on the stoop was when thick black mist poured out of the keyhole of the front door to pool at her feet. It swished around her, and when she noticed, she joined her group on the grass.

An interesting story to the knocking that is not ghost related was when Lindsay herself had knocked on it once to show what Jenny heard in the story she was telling. A guard was in the kitchen and heard it. With the history of knocks being heard in the house and on the front door, he cautiously got up and went to the window to peer out. He was never gladder to learn it was her that had done the knocking!

Another time, several people in Jenny's group saw a shadow moving independently on the house. Wondering what they were staring at, she turned to look and saw it, too. It ran away, heading toward the light. It did not vanish.

Another guide, Kelly got caught in some bizarre photos. One had gray mist swooping down on her like a bird of prey. On another tour, Kelly had a little girl about 10 to 12 years old in the group. This girl told her she never saw any ghosts where she came from, which was Florida. She said that Florida was ghost-free. Someone took a picture of Kelly and the little girl who Kelly allowed to stand by her on the porch. The weird thing about the photo? Neither she nor the little girl had a head! Instead a misty blackness had replaced the heads. In the next photo, all was back to normal.

A man had set up his camera to take a picture every ten seconds. In most of the photos nothing seemed out of the ordinary, except for one. In this picture, Kelly is alone by a window…for the whole group had disappeared!

In a photo that one boy in another group took, he got a man in a tricorn hat looking out of a window when no one was in the house. Instead of the man as a shadow, he got the photo in reverse, where the man was all in white!

Other photos captured of the house by ghost walk groups had it looking like Christmas lights blazing, with many orbs. One time, an orange ball of light was in another photograph.

I did catch several orbs with my camera…and one black shadow in the second-story left-hand window!

Touring the House

About a few weeks later, Bill and I returned to Colonial Williamsburg on a Friday to take a tour of the inside of the house. Our group and the one after us were hurried through, as they had a camera crew about to take over to film a commercial for Colonial Williamsburg. Our guide led us upstairs and I stopped to snap a picture of the bedroom at the top of the stairs. I found out later I did catch an orb in there. She took us to the middle of the room to tell us about slavery. Bill had the recorder to catch what she said. I took a few more pictures of a bedroom behind us, and then stood to listen, too. That's when things got weird. A cold crept over my hands, which grew colder and colder until they were bone-chilling cold! Then it slid up to my arms, but nowhere else on my body. My hair began to rise on my arms. I never saw it stand up that high before. I thought, 'Someone's trying to get my attention.'

Suddenly, I felt an electric snap like you feel after walking across a rug wearing a sweater and the cold left and my hair settled down. Funny thing, there were only hardwood floors in that room.

I walked over to Bill to get the recorder and found it was shut off. Upset, I asked him about it; he looked confused and said that he had turned it on and didn't understand how it turned off. Had one of the spirits in the house do this? Interesting question. I turned it on the catch the rest of the guide's talk.

Later, besides the orb in the bedroom to the right at the top of the stairs, I caught a purple anomaly on the Randolph portrait. The others I took of the same picture came out normal. I can't explain it. Even if it were a backfire from my camera light, it would be white, as that has happened many times before to me, not purple.

The next time, you stroll by the Peyton Randolph house don't be surprised if you glance at a window and find someone staring back at you! Especially when you know no one is in the building!

Besides an abundance of orbs, a shadow appeared in the upper floor window (on the left side) at the Peyton Randolph House.

Room on second floor where I had my experience.

An odd purple light is seen on this portrait of Peyton Randolph at the Peyton Randolph House.

BRICK HOUSE

The Brick House Tavern, built in 1760, is used today for those wishing to lodge right in the Historic Area, instead of at one of Colonial Williamsburg's hotels. Located on Duke of Gloucester Street, the tavern has sixteen rooms; all have private, full baths. The Brick House has always been used as lodging. In 1770, the innkeeper, Mary Davis, advertised "12 or 14 very good lodging rooms" and also noted that the first-floor rooms were reserved for ladies and the rooms above for gentlemen. That meant that for the price, you were entitled to a meal and a place to sleep. That did not mean you would have a private room, not even a private bed for that matter. The standard price meant you would be sleeping with perfect strangers, in the same bed, in a room that would house about twenty people. If you had enough money to pay for "private accommodation," you could sleep alone in your bed, but there would be multiple beds in the same room.

There is a Great Room with a fireplace in the cellar. The first floor has eight rooms. There are three queen beds, two double beds, and three twin beds. The second floor has eight rooms. There are two rooms with double beds, four with twin beds, and two with queen beds.

There's a story of a guest who reported she heard the stamping sound of boots as they walked through the front door, into her room, and then out through the gabled roof. Before that, twenty years ago, one woman woke up to someone stomping around the room, sounding like on carpeting. Problem with that, there's only bare wood floors in the building. The stomping went up to the door to her room, the door opened and shut, the stomping continued to the front door, where it opened and shut, the thing stomping out.

That was not the only ghostly phenomenon experienced at the place. Two sisters stay there every year, but never in any of the Colonial houses in the Historic Area. Since they want to remain anonymous, "A" and "B" will replace their names.

About a couple of years ago, they came as they always do and stayed at the Brick House. They climbed the stairs to their room, which was in the back of the building. Both sisters caught a very strong, very sweet odor of tobacco. Sister A knew the smell as she smoked a pipe, though she never used the kind that the odor belonged to. Both sisters thought it very strange, considering the place to be a non-smoking building, too. They got to their room, dropped their things off, and then went out to enjoy the historic district.

The next incident that happened to them was when they got ready for bed at night. Sister B lay in bed, while her sister brushed her teeth in the bathroom. Sister B glanced at the window when her sister turned off the light to come to bed and saw the silhouette of a man walk past it. Thinking it might be her imagination, Sister B went to sleep after Sister A crawled into her bed. Very early the next morning, she woke up to the sound of keys jangling. She stared at the door to the room and thought that someone was trying to get into their room. Then she realized that the sound did not come from outside, but right at the foot of her bed! She didn't want to scare her sister, so she kept it to herself.

Next night, Sister A woke up to a thump on her bed. It was followed by a thump by her feet, a thump by her leg, a thump by her knee, a thump by her thigh, a thump by her waist…until whatever made them was by her shoulder. She opened her mouth to scream. A heavy pressure lay on her chest. She remained that way for a few minutes when the pressure eased and she finally managed a squeak. All Sister B did was roll over to ask her, "Did you hear a scream?"

Sister A replied, "That was me!"

The sisters told each other of the strange things that happened to them in the room. They also felt something was still in the room with them. Sister A leaped out of bed to dash across the room to hit the light switch. Light flooded the room. Sister B saw a silvery-gray mass in the middle of the room. It rose up to the ceiling, racing across it, and passed through the wall to the room next-door. After that episode, they kept the bathroom light on at night and slept undisturbed for the rest of their stay.

On the ghost walk, Lindsay mentioned that it was thought that only the back of the building is haunted. At the time she told this to the group she had, the entire building had been rented out to a group of teachers. A couple of them sat on the front stoop. One blurted out that the whole place was haunted!

Faucets were played with, lights turned on and off with no one touching the switches, and some people complained of what they termed as "man's stink." One woman woke up to find a man in breeches and checkered shirt with greasy, straggly long hair stood by her. She thought he seemed pathetic and felt sorry for him — until he leaned over as if trying to kiss her. Being sorry for anyone, even a ghost, only went so far.

Tired of boring hotel rooms and want to try something different when staying at Colonial Williamsburg? Why not stay at the Brick House? Just don't be surprised if something unseen decides to get into bed with you. After all, the place in the eighteenth century said that up to seven people could share a bed. It would seem that they still like to do that!

The Brick House Tavern during the day.

The Brick House Tavern during the Tavern Ghost Walk.

MARKET SQUARE TAVERN

The Market Square Tavern is located on the Duke of Gloucester Street, next to Market Square and the Magazine. It has operated as a place of lodging since the eighteenth century. There are eleven rooms in all. Market Square Tavern was home to Thomas Jefferson during his law studies with George Wythe. He rose early and studied next to the window until the sun's first rays outshone his chamber stick.

There is a Great Room with a fireplace on the first floor that is considered to be original to the place. There are six rooms on the first floor and five rooms on the second floor. All the rooms have private baths.

In 1749, John Dixon leased the grounds from Williamsburg and built a store. Later on, Thomas Craig leased the building and used it as a lodging house. In 1771, Gabriel Maupin took over the lodging house. When it was renovated in 1931 and 1932, the second floor was replaced to restore the tavern to its original appearance, as remodeling done to it in the nineteenth century had almost destroyed its colonial architecture.

During the Civil War, Charles Waller and his family owned the tavern. A Rebel sympathizer, he foolishly crawled out of his sickbed to yell out the window, "Kill them, kill them," to Confederate General Henry Wise and his men as they battled Union troops. Unfortunately for Charles, the Federal troops retook the town and they remembered how he called out when that skirmish happened. Angry, they busted through the door of the tavern and surged into the building. They destroyed everything in the place and killed Charles Waller himself. Only Mrs. Waller and her infant escaped when she leapt from the second-story landing.

Over the years those staying at the place complained of tapping noises waking them at night. They say the sounds appear to be coming from outside the walls, which is strange as the room that was Charles's is on the second story. There are those who also comment that they thought the sounds came from inside the room! Suddenly, the tapping ceased early in the twenty-first century.

There are other hauntings, due to the grounds between the tavern and the magazine, too. Once the spot where the Greek Revival Church had stood, it was the scene of horror during the Civil War. The church was one of many buildings in the area turned into a makeshift hospital after the Battle of Williamsburg. Decaying flesh filled the church with foul odor and amputated arms and legs piled up in a corner.

When the Northern doctors arrived, one of them was the head surgeon. Nicknamed the "Head Devil," he drank all day and brutalized his patients. He had amputations done that were not needed. These body parts were buried in the ground. Over two hundred bodies were buried in a mass grave — and are still believed to be buried there today. It was a hellhole of a place.

The church no longer stands on the grounds, but some say cries of anguish are heard at night. Spirits of wounded soldiers are seen roaming the place.

One family, the Harrisons, stayed in the Market Square Tavern in 1992. The window of their room looked out on the grounds. One night, they saw a man digging in the dirt, right beneath their window. Not sure who he was, suddenly they realized he was dressed in a Confederate uniform. They thought he was an actor at first…until they noticed he only had one arm.

When they asked the clerk the next morning if anything was going on last night, they were told nothing at all. They learned the identity of the man later that night when they took a ghost tour — he had to be one of the many soldiers operated on.

During the day, the grounds look peaceful. At least, it seems to me every time we are there in Colonial Williamsburg, but maybe at night things change…for there are those still searching for an arm or leg taken from them.

Next time you decide to stay at the Market Square Tavern, don't be surprise if you awaken to tapping sounds or stare outside your window and see a soldier digging in the ground. It's only the ghosts that still haunt the area.

Market Square Tavern.

CARTER'S GROVE

Before Carter's Grove was built, Native Americans lived there. Artifacts that date back thousands of years have been discovered by archeologists on digs there. In the early eighteenth century, Robert "King" Carter purchased the land. The boat builder, shipper, investor, moneylender, and tobacco planter was to become the richest man in Virginia. He owned 1,000 slaves and forty-four tobacco plantations and amassed 300,000 acres of land. Descendents of his include two presidents, three men who signed the Declaration of Independence, and even Robert E. Lee was a descendent from him.

When he passed away, the property went to his daughter, Elizabeth, and his grandson, Carter Burwell, when he turned twenty-one. Carter's will also provided that "this estate in all times to come to be called and to go by the name of Carter's Grove." Burwell started construction on the Georgian mansion in 1750 that stands on the property today. He only lived in the house for six months. He died in May 1756 at age 41. Burwell's son Nathaniel inherited the property when he came of age on April 15, 1771. He graduated from the College of William and Mary, and married Susannah Grymes. Susannah bore him seven children. Five of them survived infancy. She died in 1788. Her husband, now a widower, took for his second wife widow Lucy Page Taylor in 1789. He fathered eight more children with her. They moved to Carter Hall in Clarke County, where Nathaniel passed away in 1814.

Carter's Grove remained in the Burwells' hands until 1838, when the family sold it to Thomas Wynne. Eight more owners owned the place before Archibald and Mollie McCrea from Lawrenceville, Virginia, bought it on January 21, 1928. The home was in a terrible state. In a patriotic mood, one occupant had painted some of the paneling red, white, and blue. Chickens lived in the basement and they found a hole in the hall ceiling. The McCreas fixed it up and threw many grand parties. Mrs. McCrea died in 1960. The Rockefeller family charitable trust acquired it in 1964. The estate ended up with Colonial Williamsburg in 1969.

By accident, they discovered a seventeenth century settlement on the property in the 1970s. This was Martin's Hundred (hundred defined a subdivision of an English county), or also known as Wolstenholme Towne. It was named for Richard Martin, recorder of the City of London, who was its owner. Sir John Wolstenholme was among its investors.

When Carter purchased the land, there had been no evidence that a tragedy had taken place. At least 220 men and women braved the ocean in 1618 to arrive and settle the land about six miles from Jamestown; 140 of them survived while others died off from starvation or disease by 1622. More settlers came. On March 22, 1622, the Powhatan Indians, who lived nearby, massacred 400 of them. The uprising or revolt worked for the Indians — by 1645, the settlement was abandoned with the remaining settlers moving to Jamestown. Two graves discovered are linked to the 1622 uprisings. A body of a man whose skull had been holed by a blow (perhaps from a spade) between the eyes was unearthed in one grave. In a trash pit, the remains of a woman curled up on her side had been uncovered.

When Carter, his son, and grandson owned the place, both the affluent and poor lived in Williamsburg. Since only about five percent of the population could live well, most of the residents lived in one-room dwellings that contained dirt floors. Slaves, which were half of the population at the time, lived in shacks or overcrowded buildings. Slaves' marriages were not legal in the eyes of their white owners, which allowed the owners to sell off children from mothers or husbands from wives and vice versa without a qualm. A slave worked fourteen hours. They may have had only Sundays off. When money grew tight, owners rented out their slaves, too. This happened to two slaves from Carter's Grove, Jim and Betty, along with their three children.

Jim worked in the gardens of the Governor's Palace from sun-up to sunset. He knew that late Saturday he would be able to leave to spend time with his family on Sunday, but one rainy Saturday night after he got back to Carter's Grove, he found that his wife and children had been rented off. During his free time, he searched for them, but never found them. He died a lonely man.

It seems that he still is searching for his family, even after death. In the 1970s, an employee saw a dark-skinned man walk out of the woods one Saturday afternoon, after the plantation had closed. He thought that maybe the man's car had broken down and he called out to him, but the man walked past him. Instead the man headed back to the woods. The employee looked for him, but it was if the man had vanished with no trace. That was when he remembered the stories told of Jim's ghost seen on the grounds.

Paul Kline and his family from Canada were driving along Old Country Road to Williamsburg from Carter's Grove when they saw a man walking in the street. He wore clothing just like the actors back at the plantation. Kline rolled down his window and called out for the man to move from the road. The man did, staring at the ground. When Kline looked back over his shoulder to see the man, he saw that he no longer stood there. As if like a dream, he had dissipated.

Last of all there is a tale of three pirates buried in the cellar at Carter's Grove. It is claimed that their ghosts still hold a card game there every now and then.

Where once one could tour the property, for now, according to the website, Colonial Williamsburg have closed it while they conduct a comprehensive assessment of Wolstenholme Towne on the property. To know when it reopens to the public, keep tabs on the website link: http://www.history.org/Almanack/places/hb/hbcgrove.cfm.

OTHER GHOSTLY TALES
OF COLONIAL WILLIAMSBURG

You Can't Arrest Ghosts

This story happened in Colonial Williamsburg. Close to nighttime, the police got a call about a disturbance not far from the Historic Area. The story goes that when they arrived, they found this man and woman dressed in clothing from another era standing with their backs turned to them. The couple carried bags. The police thought that maybe these were costumed interpreters and decided to drive past them. As they drove past, one of the policemen in the car saw the two people disappear into thin air. They searched the area, but found no one.

She Died On the Street

There was a girl, around fifteen years old. She came from a rich family, but the man she loved came from a poor family so they would not allow her to marry him. The young couple decided they were going to run away together and get married. The boy was in the place where he was supposed to meet her, which was down the street from her house. The girl packed her bags and snuck out of the house. She was running down the street when she thought about how much trouble she would be in. She decided not to run away, but to go back home. She ran back down the street, leaving her love behind. She looked back to make sure he was not following her. Suddenly, she was run over by a carriage and died on the spot.

The ghost story connected with this came into play when a woman snapped a picture with their cell phone of a family member holding a lantern during a ghost walk. When they got to the next location of the tour she showed the picture. Instead of the young man holding the lantern as it should have been, the photo had a black mist over most of the picture. You couldn't see the person in the picture, but the lantern light was blurred across the screen. The woman let the guide see it and the guide said that happened many other times at that spot.

Bruton Parish Graveyard

One of the legends of the church's graveyard concerns a preacher, a very charismatic man. His wife had become ill and was at death's door. He told her he would love her forever. Forever only lasted one year after her death. The preacher married a beautiful and very wealthy woman who owned land next-door to the church. When his second wife died, he put her grave between his first wife's and the plot that would be his gravesite when he passed away. It is said that the first wife, dressed in gray, haunts the spot, still angry that not only was her husband faithless, but that he dared to put his second wife between them in death.

Bruton Parish Church.

A tomb in the Bruton Parish Cemetery — check out the skull and crossbones!

Bruton Parish Church is on Duke of Gloucester Street and is a working parish. The church was founded in 1654. It was the church for many visiting dignitaries of colonial times, including Thomas Jefferson and George Washington.

The church is open during the day for tourists. The graves are the most intriguing attraction at the churchyard and they exemplify colonial styles of grave art and funeral customs. These graves date back to the 1600s and 1700s. The church and its grounds are not open at night, but the church is on a corner and it is easy enough to find a quiet spot to stand next to the gate or wall to set an EVP recorder or experiment with night photography. The church's website is http://www.brutonparish.org.

Orrel House

A guest of the Orrel House, built in 1810, reported supernatural hi-jinks, including the water being turned on in the downstairs bathroom, a broken glass, and an upstairs bathroom wrapped in toilet paper, like a Halloween prank.

The Orrel House is located on East Francis Street and the main drive for the Williamsburg Inn. Little is known about the structure prior to the 1800s since records were destroyed during the Civil War. John Orrell bought the property in the early 1800s and lived in the house for about twenty years. The builder of the house was very practical because the unusually steep lower slope of the gambrel roof allowed more headroom and floor space on the second floor.

The Tale of the Clock That Stopped

Russell Simons was looking for a job in Virginia and stayed at a boarding house. One night, he was awakened one night and saw a transparent monochromatic female specter with dark hair floating inches from the floor. The next morning, he discovered his alarm clock had stopped and mentioned this to the owner of the place. The owner told him the story of the time he visited the hospital where he wife was. She had passed away there. When he returned home, he found all clocks, except for one, stopped when she died. He bought new ones. These too, also stopped working for no reason. He pointed to an antique clock hanging over a mantel, one of his wife's prized family heirlooms. It was the only one that didn't stop. Then he showed Simons a picture of the deceased wife. To Simons' shock, the apparition he saw in the bedroom was the owner's wife!

Tayloe House

Though the Revolutionary War is long gone, there are still spirits of Patriots haunting many of the grounds of homes in the Williamsburg area. One of these is the Tayloe House. Though built for Dr. James Carter, who did live there for a time, it became the home of Colonel Tayloe in 1759. He had an office on the grounds with an unusual bell-shaped roof. Never touched like his well-manicured lawns, the woods behind his home grew wild. During the fight for freedom many patriots camped out in those woods, feeling safe from anyone seeing them.

Centuries later, sounds of laughter and voices and the odor of campfires came from the woods behind the house. One tourist couple heard the sounds of merriment and seeing the bonfire walked around to the back of the house — only to find the area dark and empty of life.

Whether an intelligent haunting or just a residual from the past, it seems those who fought in the Revolutionary War are still camping out.

Ogle Still Haunting Nicholson House

Cuthbert Ogle, a well-known violinist from the mid-1700s, lived in the Nicholson House. He fell in love with the structure once it came up for sale and resided in the home until his death in the year of 1755. Apparently, death hasn't kept him from remaining there. For he is blamed for people's shoulders being touched and the loud scratching noises heard at night.

Or could it be Robert Nicholson, the man who built the house and took in boarders for many years? Sometimes, a legend will say one thing, until a paranormal investigator comes along to disprove it, with another name on an EVP, or digging up the history. Whoever is behind the ghostly goings on, the stories persist.

You can find the Nicholson House on York Street in Williamsburg. It is now a bed and breakfast.

Chapter Three

YORK COUNTY

York County is part of the Virginia Peninsula. Not far from Williamsburg and James City County, it is one of the historical areas that make up the Historic Triangle. Historic Yorktown lies in its borders, along with the Yorktown Battlefield that saw not only the Revolutionary War, but later on, battles of the War Between the States, too. Besides the tourism, thanks to the battlefield, plantations, Yorktown, and more, there's a bustling town that residents reside in today, many unaware of the ghosts that still haunt there.

It was here at Cape Henry that John Smith and the first colonists to the New World landed on April 26, 1607. These same colonists established the first permanent English settlement, Jamestown, on May 14, 1607. There is a cross marking the moment of their landing, erected by the National Society Daughters of the American Colonists in 1935. This was in memory of the wooden cross that those long-ago colonists put up.

Not far offshore from Cape Henry is where a sea battle happened during the Revolutionary War. Two mighty war fleets exchanged cannon shots for about two and a half hours. Thanks to Admiral Comte deGrasse, commander of the French fleet sent to aid General George Washington, the British were stopped from relieving Lord Cornwallis at Yorktown. This led to victory at Yorktown, which eventually ended the war on October 19, 1781, and set the stage for a new government and nation.

The Yorktown Victory Center chronicles America's evolution from colonial status to nationhood through a unique blend of timeline, film, great exhibits set to themes, and outdoor living history. My husband, Bill, and I were fortunate enough to be there when some of the park staff in costume showed us how cannons were shot off and the consequences of this part of the battle. It was a place we would need to go back to in the much warmer summertime when we had more time to enjoy the facilities.

Or you can drive down to the Yorktown Battlefield and see where it all happened — and where people claim the spirits of those who perished in battle still carry on the fight today.

Just as the ghosts of those who lived in nearby plantations, houses, and even a bed and breakfast still haunt the homes they had lived in when alive. They are joined by the phenomenon of a certain infamous bridge on a quiet wooded road and much more.

York County is chock full of hauntings... Do you dare to learn about them?

CREEPY CRAWFORD ROAD

"Searchers after horror haunt strange, far places." — H. P. Lovecraft

Crawford Road is in York County, though it also is in Newport News, too. Strangely enough, the spelling is different, depending on what area you live in.

There are assorted legends surrounding the bridge that crosses over Crawford Road. One of them talks of African Americans who were hanged at the location. This particular legend goes on to say that an African American woman in a white dress has been seen standing on top of the bridge, right at the edge. Then, right before the witnesse's eyes, she falls from it and vanishes just before making contact with the pavement. At other times, she halts in mid-air and begins to swing back and forth, as if hanging by a rope.

There are a couple of stories to explain some of these hauntings. One suggests that a young black bride fled her wedding and hanged herself from the bridge to escape an undesired fate of being married to a man she did not care for. Other suggested folklore mentions that she was hanged there because of her color. There is a story that a few black men were hanged from the bridge by the KKK for a Klan statement. I can tell you there is plenty of KKK graffiti scribbled on the bridge and on the road as you drive up to the bridge. Though I suspect that these are more the work of teenagers thinking it is funny than as a KKK statement, African Americans' ghosts have been sighted. There have been reports of Civil War soldiers seen, too. Besides sightings, some witnesses have heard disembodied voices and strange knocking noises.

Crawford Road Bridge during the daytime.

However, the strangest stories are those about people's vehicles that stop running as they approach the bridge. In many of these tales, those in the car have to get out and push past the "haunted" bridge. Not all cars need to be pushed, though. Some say that their car shifts into neutral and will roll some distance. Afterwards, the drivers get out and discover what looks like handprints all over the paint. Sometimes though, the motor refuses to start and the driver has to call a tow truck to come get them and their vehicle. Would you like to have a disabled car by the bridge at night, waiting until a tow truck finally comes? I wouldn't.

These are not the only weird tales about this very haunted area, or the bridge itself. A friend of mine had been told by a coworker that years ago a man had his car "carjacked" by a killer who forced him to take money from his cash flow teller somewhere in Newport News and then have him drive at gunpoint to the remote area of Crawford Road. Once they got there, the killer murdered the poor man and dumped his body at the bridge. Does his specter now haunt the bridge, too?

More bizarre stories center on a building off in the woods nearby. Before you come to the bridge, there's a fenced-off road that actually heads back into a clearing. An abandoned building with no doors stands in the clearing. Suddenly, red eyes may appear in one of the open doorways and watch you. When you draw closer to the building, the red eyes vanish. An eerie feeling of something watching has overtaken those who do enter the place. There are claims of some film that caught a shadow moving along the walls (always in the shape of a tall male creeping along), but I have never found any evidence of any such film, even on YouTube. There have also been reports of people feeling like they have had their feet stepped on, voices whispering, and something touching the middle of their backs. Both during the daytime and at night when my husband and I were there, I never attempted to find this building. I couldn't be sure that I wouldn't be trespassing.

KKK on Crawford Road, just before the bridge.

Other scary tales tell of a strange black truck that appears and begins to give chase. It looks like it's about to catch up with the back of the vehicle it is pursuing when it disappears. Someone e-mailed me to tell me his scary experience with a truck that happened on March 14, 2010. He has asked to remain anonymous.

He had been driving with someone else along Crawford Road and said they never ran into any other vehicle. Just as they drove beneath the bridge it seemed that out of nowhere a truck appeared right behind them with his high beams on. The truck began to flash its headlights. Suddenly, the headlights went off. The truck had vanished. Though scared, they turned around and headed back where they had come from, but never found the truck.

Another creepy tale concerns a couple of young men who drove down the road one night. They had just gone beneath the bridge when it sounded like they had run over something on the cement. They pulled over to the side of the road and went back to check to see if they had indeed run over some poor animal or something else. They found nothing. So they climbed back into the car and proceeded away from the bridge. That's when things got freaky. The windows fogged up, and the next thing they saw were handprints making their way up the windows from the outside. When the handprints reached the top of the windshield, they heard a loud thud from the roof of the car, as if something was trying to get in through the roof. The thudding noise stopped and then they heard a smearing noise and the back window looked like someone had fallen off the top of the car and slid down the window. Another bump resounded on the top of the trunk and then they heard the sound again hit the road behind them. Scared, they turned off the motor, got out, and checked to see what it could have been. Once again, of course, there was nothing. Could this be a residue reenactment of the murder victim that my friend learned about?

Was that enough of an experience for them to not drive down Crawford Road at night? No. They were driving around a few years later, listening to a CD they had burnt, and turned onto Crawford Road. Everything was fine until they reached the bridge. When they slipped under it, a high-pitched squealing issued from the track they were listening to on the CD. The noise lasted for about ten seconds until they drove well away from the bridge. What freaked them out was the CD had been fine all night — until they approached the bridge. Later on, they also discovered that the noise had been forever imprinted on that particular track.

More legends that concern the haunted area are that something appears out of nowhere in front of a moving car and drivers swerve to avoid it. They stop the vehicle and get out, but find nothing. Of course, a deer can quickly leap out of the woods and bolt across the road to disappear into the brush on the other side, or even an owl or a bat could fly across the road. This story could be easily explained away — except when you are there at night, the creepiness of the area makes you doubt the logical reasons.

There have been paranormal groups that have investigated this area. They have gotten EVPs and photographs, too. Have any of them ever figured out the truth? Not as far as I have seen.

Another person who commented on my blog said that she had lived in Newport News for a couple of years before moving back to Southampton County. Her boyfriend and she had visited Crawford Road, aka Crybaby Bridge, a few times. In one photograph they had taken, they noticed a smoky figure of what looked to be a woman in a long dress. They also once caught sight of headlights from some vehicle. The headlights dissipated.

Another witness had gone there one time with her husband to check out if the stories were true. She did get some orbs in her pictures. Nothing else though happened.

Patty Ceran went there during April 2008 with her husband Dean. They drove under the bridge and kept going. After driving a few minutes and the road not coming out anywhere, she told Dean to turn around so they could go back the way the other way. After crossing underneath the overpass again, she made him stop so she could take some pictures. In her first photo, she got a bright white light. She was in front of the bridge and standing beside the car and there was no one else on the road either way. She wondered where the light came from.

The Author's Visit to the Bridge

I decided this time around to find the road for myself. After much searching on the Internet, I found directions to it, thanks to a paranormal investigating group. There was even a picture of it in the daylight so I could be sure that we found the right bridge. My husband and trusty sidekick, Bill, put in Crawford Road and the nearby cross street of Tour Road into the GPS and we left Chesterfield during the day to find it. Well, we did. It reminded me of the Bunnyman Bridge, except it was covered in graffiti.

A few cars drove past us. A woman pulled over to talk to me as she wondered why I was taking pictures of the bridge. She had decided to drive down the road as her husband used to like doing it when he was alive. During the daytime, it is a lonely stretch of road with plenty of woods on both sides of it, but even in the day, the bridge appears creepy.

Orbs on and by Crawford Road Bridge at night.

I took pictures, used my voice recorder, and then we left. I admit the place bothered me during the day and I was glad to see the back of it — except I knew I had to return later to get pictures at when it was dark and to see if I could catch EVPs.

We did return at night on January 2, 2010. The temperature was bone-chilling cold. We had left our friend Paul Knight's house in Norfolk after dropping off his belated Christmas gift. We found the bridge again and this time Bill drove beneath it and pulled the car over to the side of the road a few feet away. He remained in the car while I stepped outside of the car with my equipment.

I started to walk towards the bridge, but halted a few feet away. Something inside me wouldn't let me draw any closer than I had to. The place had creeped me out in the daylight, but this time it unnerved me. Still I had pictures to take and that's just what I did. After I felt I'd done enough, I switched off my camera. I brought out my new KII EMF meter I had gotten for Christmas. It had done well at Champlain earlier, but I got nothing with it here. I stuck it back in my bookbag and withdrew my digital recorder. I asked if anyone was there and wanted to communicate with me to let me know. A loud crack vibrated in the air from one side of the bridge. I paused. Of course, it might have been an animal or a branch had snapped off. Logically, I told myself that, but the unnerved me wondered. I did this for a few minutes more; talked again, waited, and then shut it off. I put it away and headed back to the car...all the while mindful of the weird vibes the bridge gave off behind me. I climbed back into the car and we drove off. I stared at the bridge through the back window. Relief filled me when we got back to the Newport News area, found the on-ramp to I-64, and zoomed down the highway to find the railroad crossing where the Cohoke Light had been seen.

It was later, after the photos were uploaded into my laptop and the recording into my husband's PC, that I got the troubling results. Several orbs were in a few photos; one of them shining bright and sitting on the side of the road not far from where I had stood. Another had a single orb on top of the bridge where supposedly the phantom of the African American woman is seen before she drops. What spooked me, though, was the recording. Mostly it was silent, except for that loud crack, when a low voice said a single word. A couple seconds later, I thought I said the same word, but before sending this book off to my publisher, I listened to it again. I realized, after replaying that single word over and over, what it was. It said, "Mommy." Least that is what it sounded like to me. What I said had seemed the same, but wasn't. Still, why mommy? I don't know. Will I ever go back to the bridge? Maybe. I'll be sure to bring a load of investigators with me if I do decide to return there.

Next time you decide to go barreling down Crawford Road at night, beware when you come upon the bridge... There are unseen things hanging around there, just waiting to scare the unwary living.

A HOUSE CALLED "VERANDAH"

A friend of mine who lives in Newport News gave me the e-mail address of a friend of hers who had lived in a haunted house in York County some time ago. This friend now lives out west. I sent the woman an e-mail and got an answer from her not long after. She wrote eight pages about what happened to her and her husband when they lived in that house they had bought. Now before I go on, I was asked not to reveal her real name, so I will call her by the fictitious name of "Millie."

The first time Millie saw the house she gasped. She and her husband had been fruitlessly searching for a place for two days and had been about to give up when the Realtor gave them a call about this house.

It was more beautiful than Millie expected — everything that a gracious home in the Virginia countryside should look like. Painted in gray/blue, with accents of burgundy and white, it had a covered porch that wrapped almost all the way around it. Holly, boxwood, and azaleas surrounded the house like Indians around a covered wagon. The white front porch swing added the perfect touch to a place that symbolized Southern loveliness.

Not a place that could ever be haunted... Or could it?

The first thing Millie noticed as they entered the house was a painting that hung over the brick fireplace. It was of the house itself. Her one thought at that moment was that someone must love the place very much to have a painting done of it, but the house didn't have that warm feeling about it. She caught sight of heavy mauve-colored drapes, and when she drew them back, she found a set of French doors. As she swept the entire room with her eyes, she saw floor-to-ceiling glass windows, all with views of a large backyard ringed by oak trees.

She asked the Realtor, "Why would anyone want to cover up these windows to hide such a view?"

The Realtor couldn't give her an answer.

The next thing Millie noticed was the largest bible she ever saw sitting on a heavy oak stand that reminded her of a pulpit. It faced the kitchen and not the lovely view of the backyard. She thought it odd at the time.

She and her husband met the sellers the day of the house inspection. The husband was a big, burly man with an air of cold authority about him. The wife never looked at them the entire time, but instead kept folding some clothing. She must not have made much of an impression as Millie couldn't remember much of what she looked like, but she did remember that the woman did not want to sell the house. They had lived in it for years and their children had grown up in it, but the kids were gone and the husband wanted to move to a golf course condo. When closing day rolled around, the Realtor told Millie and her husband that the wife wouldn't be coming. She was too upset about selling the place.

The first thing Millie did when they moved in was to discard the heavy curtains from all the windows in the living room and dining room. It lifted the closed-in feeling the house had and lightened up the place... That was when the strange occurrences began to happen.

Their washing machine lid would not stay closed. Millie would be doing the laundry and, when she would not hear it run, would discover the lid up and the washing stopped in mid-cycle. This kept happening over and over again. She tried shaking the machine with the lid down, but it never snapped up. Filled with laundry, empty, running, or in OFF position, the lid remained closed for her on these tests.

There was one bedroom on the second floor that always overcame her with sadness. She thought, 'Someone spent a lot of time crying here.' Could this have been the wife who did not want to sell the house? Or something or someone else?

One afternoon, as she straightened up the bedroom, sounds of cannons booming, horses neighing, gunshots, and men yelling reached her ears from outside the house. Maybe it was the historic plantation a few miles away hosting a Civil War re-enactment (I found this had to be Endview since her house bordered its land). She called the plantation's office, but was told nothing was going on that day. Living in a place steeped in history from the Revolutionary War to the Civil War, one can imagine the ghostly battles still going on.

Virginia, whether summer or winter, is always damp and humid, but the summertime was always worse, due to insects. Millie worked hard to keep the place cleaned and picked up, especially the kitchen and dining room. It would have not done to have ants and other pests become a problem, attracted by any food left out.

One morning she walked into the dining room and found a half-emptied glass of water in the middle of the dining room table. She knew she hadn't left it there. As for anyone else, her husband was out of town on business and they didn't have any children. Had something of the supernatural persuasion decided they needed a glass of water to drink? Or did they just want to irritate her?

Phenomena that happened repeatedly in the dining room were the nasty smell of flatulence, followed by what sounded like young men laughing. She thought that maybe the smell came from their aging dog. Except neither he nor the other dog they owned was in the area whenever these occurrences happened. Also, despite that the dining room was warm and sunny, neither dog wanted to linger there. In fact, the older dog would stop just short of the doorway and could never be persuaded to go any further.

Pranks were pulled on her. One night, as she got ready to go to a party, she looked for her powder makeup compact where she always kept it: on the counter in the master bathroom. She couldn't find it. She asked her husband if he'd seen it. He hadn't. He entered the bathroom to check, but never saw a sign of it either. They searched the bedroom and then checked the bathroom one more time. To their surprise, they found the compact on the counter. They looked at each other and he said, "I know it wasn't there when we looked."

Millie decided to investigate the house's history. She, along with two friends, went to the plantation. No tours were being done at that time and they had the manager all to themselves. The manager told them that the house and its land had been part of the plantation originally. Slaves used to farm tobacco and, later, grain on the land. The pond at the end of their road was used by the slaves to water the plantation's mules.

Plus, during the War Between the States, hundreds of soldiers had encamped there. A neighbor of theirs had built his garage on his lot adjacent to theirs and discovered rusted parts of a gun, bullets, and buttons. All of this stuff dated from the Civil War.

Knowing the history explained a lot of things that Millie experienced. It helped her some, too. Life for a while seemed quiet.

Then one afternoon, as she stood at the top of the stairs, she felt that someone or something stood behind her, that this very same "something" wanted to push her down the stairs. Frightened, she grabbed the handrail and bolted downstairs. She yelled, "That's ENOUGH! You are SCARING me. PLEASE STOP." She wondered if she was losing her mind.

The next day she kept a hair appointment. The stylist who did her hair was one she never met before. They talked. The stylist seemed friendly and helpful. Then for no reason whatsoever, Millie blurted out that her house was haunted. Of course, she felt stupid and embarrassed.

The stylist put down the comb she held. She told Millie that she believed in ghosts and was a member of a paranormal investigating group. The group had investigated places in Yorktown and Newport News, like the graveyard in old Yorktown, a church, and around the battlefields. She offered the services of her group to check out Millie's home.

Millie agreed to the investigation. She and her husband left on their vacation and their two dogs were placed in a boarding kennel for the duration. The group set up both audio and visual equipment in the house. One camera on a tripod was positioned at the top of the stairs. Audio equipment was situated in the bedroom, while downstairs, they placed a tape recorder.

They found something all right. When Millie returned to Virginia, they presented her with what they collected. On tape they captured sounds of bugles being blown and cannons being fired. They had also caught the laughter of what sounded like three young men. The researchers also had first-hand experiences, like the unpleasant odor in the kitchen.

As for the camera upstairs, no ghostly images or full-bodied apparitions were caught — but they did get something that gave everyone goosebumps. The hallway bobbed up and down while something kept tapping on the camera, almost in a playful manner.

After that, nothing unusual ever happened to Millie and her husband for the remainder of the time they lived there. Millie's husband retired and they moved out west. They sold the house to an English woman from London. Millie heard from former neighbors that the woman didn't live in it for long before she also put the house up for sale. It appears that the ghostly residents never left the premises, unlike the mortal ones.

CIVIL WAR STILL BEING FOUGHT

"All wars are civil wars, because all men are brothers." — Francois Fenelon

If it wasn't enough for Yorktown to be the center of the Revolutionary War at one point, years later, the War Between the States was fought there, too. President Lincoln sent McClellan and an army of 121,000 Union soldiers to Yorktown. They camped right at the trenches built by Confederates to keep them from reaching Richmond.

It was a horrible situation. Ticks, mud, and cannon fire made it difficult for both sides. Worse for the Northern troops, McClellan had them digging ditches and moving artillery around the clock.

Confederate General Magruder had his meager forces move around to fool the Union soldiers into thinking he had more men than he did. McClellan fell for it and asked Lincoln for more men. The President told him to attack. Instead McClellan took to bed, saying he was ill.

McClellan, to the irritation of some, had always insisted on thoroughness when it came to planning and preparation, and the Peninsula Campaign was no exception. He overestimated his foe's strength and suddenly, in the face of superior numbers and firepower, forfeited the ground as untenable. Around midnight of May 3, 1862, the Confederate heavy guns had ceased their diverting fire, were spiked, and left behind by the retreating army. At dawn on the May 4, the Union army discovered Yorktown abandoned. However, the Confederates had left behind a new weapon of war — land mines, which claimed the lives of several Union soldiers.

Though no one died of the actual battle itself, many soldiers did die from hypothermia and disease. Others starved to death. Due to such tragedy, there have been apparitions seen to this day. People talk of seeing men in blue and others dressed in gray marching around the colonial battlefields.

Earthworks of Yorktown Battlefield.

One witness who lives locally saw a Union soldier crawling along the field. When she mentioned it to her sister, the woman thanked her; she thought she'd also seen something like that, but thought she was crazy.

Today, there are well-preserved Union and Confederate fortifications to remind of Yorktown's Civil War history. A National Cemetery, established in 1866, contains over 2,200 interments, mostly Union dead, though not far is a small Confederate burial ground of undetermined size. The battlefields are open every day of the year except Christmas and are near the visitor's center, directly across from the Colonial Parkway. For more information, go to http://www.nps.gov/york.

Remember, if you see a Union or Confederate soldier while walking the battlefields, it's just the past reliving itself in a supernatural way.

SURRENDER FIELD

Surrender Field is where the English and German armies threw their weapons down at the feet of the American Continental Army and the French. Yorktown residents also came to watch the formal surrender. Though bitter about it all, the losing side had to do this, as the terms of surrender had been signed at Moore House on October 19, 1781. Today this historic area is a national park. Tourists walk where soldiers had marched in defeat and where others who had triumphed stood and cheered.

In 1984, one visitor to the park found the place filled with crowds. He heard drums and fifes. A familiar melody was being played. He and other tourists searched for the musicians playing it, but couldn't find them. Even stranger, they heard laughter and cheers from out of nowhere. He later learned that this has happened over and over for many years. Is this a residual of what happened that day back in 1781? Does what was felt that day manage to reach through time and space to those who stroll the park? Good question.

You can find Surrender Field, and maybe experience this yourself, by driving along Moore House Road (Route 288) to Surrender Road. If you hear the faint sound of drums that day and see a specter of an English soldier marching in sadness, don't be surprised. After all, sometimes history lives on even after death.

U.S. NAVAL WEAPONS STATION

No one saved them. Instead everyone, including the horses and the carriage, got sucked down into the swamp. From then on, they haunted the area.

When you drive past this base from I-64 along Colonial National History Parkway in Yorktown, it contains more than just the military. It has ghosts, too. Personnel of the base have reported sounds of horses struggling and women screaming. Over a century ago, Governor Edward Digges's daughter and her friends were returning in a carriage from Yorktown when suddenly the carriage ran off the road into the Black Swamp.

U.S. Naval Weapons Station provides a weapons and ammunition storage and loading facility for ships of the U.S. Atlantic Fleet. The site of the weapons station was acquired for the Navy by a presidential proclamation on August 7, 1918. At that time, it was the largest naval installation in the world, its land area covering about twenty square miles. It is rich in colonial history. The infantry of both the American Revolution and the Civil War marched on Old Williamsburg Road, which today runs through the station. The oldest structure at the Yorktown Naval Weapons Station is the Lee House, built around 1649, where many generations of the family lived out their lives before the property was acquired by the U.S. government.

It was in 1917 that Congress requested that a search for a weapons handling and storage facility on the Atlantic Coast be assumed. What was needed was a sheltered inland waterway deep enough to accommodate capital ships, along with a sparsely populated area sufficient in size to provide quantity distance separation for explosive material processing and storage facilities. The thought was that it also be close to the naval base at Norfolk, so that short boat trips for explosive loadings could be handled.

The site was found and commissioned July 1, 1918. Today, it is surrounded by fence and you have to go through guard stations to get in, but the haunts that still go through their tragedy are already inside. After all, ghosts can't be regulated by the government, can they?

CORNWALLIS'S CAVE

Lord Cornwallis occupied Yorktown, staying in the Nelson House. It was something he always did; occupy the best house in areas he and his army invaded. Unfortunately, this time, it would be his last stand. This was 1781, and the Continental army would battle the English and German forces here.

It took the combined American and French armies and a battle between the French and British fleets in the Chesapeake Bay to seal the fate of General Cornwallis and his British troops at Yorktown. From September 5-9, the French forced the British navy to retreat to New York. General Cornwallis became stranded.

During the siege, people fled to a cave off the shores of the York River to hide from bombardment from the Continental army. According to legend, Lord Cornwallis himself took shelter here; legend also says he cowered in a corner for most of the siege. Is this true? Whether this is or not, this place is called Cornwallis's Cave to this day.

Interesting note, trapped against the York River, many of the English soldiers tried to escape by swimming across its waters. Suddenly, a squall came up and swept them away, drowning many of the soldiers. How strange something like this appeared at this time, wouldn't you think? As for others of the English and German forces, they perished by artillery fire that kept coming and coming. Cornwallis had no choice but to surrender.

Bill and Mark Layne investigate Cornwallis's Cave.

Looking into Cornwallis's Cave.

Trash in one smaller cave inside Cornwallis's Cave.

The English army left, and Yorktown grew quiet for the rest of its life. Except for the legends of voices heard coming from the cave — frantic, frightened voices. It is hard for any group of people, much less one, to get inside due to metal bars across the entrance. Yet, there are those who claim to hear these voices coming from inside the cave. For some spirits, the war is still happening. Other phenomena are orbs captured in photos taken of the place.

My husband, Bill, and I were there, met by a friend, Mark Layne. We had walked through the town, pausing at Nelson House and a couple of other places, and then we went down to the shore to find the cave. We found it. I took some photographs and then drew close with my digital recorder, hoping to catch some of these spectral voices. I didn't. As for peering into the cave itself through the bars, I saw some trash inside, but not phantoms. For me that day, the voices were silent.

The next time you stroll along the river and hear frantic voices coming from Cornwallis's Cave, ignore them and keep walking. No doubt these are people long past in need of any help.

NELSON HOUSE

This is considered to be one of the most well haunted places in Yorktown. It is an imposing three-story building on Main Street. Tom Nelson, the first influential member of Yorktown, built it in 1730 to house him, his wife, Margaret, and their three children, William, Thomas and Mary. William also became a powerful politician, serving as both president of the Governor's Council and as acting governor.

After Margaret died, Tom married Francis Tucker, a widow. When the stepmother passed away in 1766, the property passed over to Tom's grandson, Thomas Nelson Jr., (1738-89), eldest of William's five sons. Nelson was given the title "Junior" to distinguish himself from his uncle, who was also named Thomas. He was Yorktown's most famous son and one of the signers of the Declaration of Independence. He died from an asthma attack six years after the revolution. His wife, Lucy, remained in the house for more than thirty years after her husband's death. The house remained in the Nelson family until 1908. During the 1862 Peninsula Campaign of the American Civil War, Yorktown was captured from the Confederacy and then used as the base for the Union Army of the Potomac under General George B. McClellan. Nelson House became a hospital for Confederate wounded and later on during the war, Northern forces.

Filled to the brim with the wounded, the odors of decaying flesh made it difficult to breathe and the windows were kept opened. The third floor held the most critically wounded. No doubt, many died, and not peacefully, in their sleep.

In 1914, Captain and Mrs. George P. Blow purchased the Nelson House and renovated it as the center of a large estate known as "York Hall." The National Park Service acquired the house in 1968 and restored it to its colonial appearance. Most of the Nelson House is original, including the bricks and most of the mortar in the outer walls. Inside the house, the wall panels and most of the wooden floors are original, a notable exception being the floor in the downstairs hall. The paint on the walls matches the color of the first paint applied after the house was constructed. The furnishings in the house today include reproductions and a few period pieces, none of which belonged to the Nelsons. Funny thing, there appears to be a cannonball still stuck in the outside walls of the place. There are even still holes put there when the Siege of Yorktown went on.

There are stories of various kinds of ghostly phenomena. Someone once put their ear to the door and swore they heard someone breathing on the other side. Next thing that happened, something punched the inside of the door. There have been reports of scents of rotting flesh, gusts of wind rushing through empty hallways, and voices when those that heard them were alone in the place. People have reported seeing apparitions of men of the Civil War era. There is an entity of a young British soldier seen at various spots around Nelson House too. The legend goes that he was killed in the secret stairway when Nelson turned the guns on his own house, or so was reported to Mrs. Blow at the time they moved in. This was from Marguerite du Pont Lee's book, *Virginia Ghosts*, which is out of print. The sound of footsteps, cold spots, tricks on the living, and playing with the lights are blamed on this apparition. Now she admitted they never saw or heard anything when she told this at a tea party of the Garden Club of Virginia when a door swung open with force against the sideboard, shattering several dishes. Mrs. Blow blamed it on a draught, but told to another guest, Mrs. Chewning later, that she found no evidence of any draft. Sobbing of a woman has also been heard coming from an empty third floor room.

Nelson House.

Some friends walked by the house late one Halloween night. As they walked by the right side of the building they watched as a third-floor window began to open. They knew no one was in the place, so imagine what they thought when moans and cries came from that window. Suddenly, a man's bloodied face peered down at them and frightened, they ran back to their car. Another instance happened to a ghost tour when the person in charge got permission by the park ranger to let them go all the way up to the third floor where normally tourists are not allowed. They saw a dark figure there, one that vanished.

I got to Yorktown and to the Nelson House in the fall of 2009. Not only was my husband with me, but also my friend Marcus Layne. I left them and started taking pictures of the house and walked around it, using my digital recorder. The place was locked up, appearing not to be open that day so I could not do a tour of it.

Whether from the Revolutionary War or the Civil War, Nelson House is haunted. If you dare to look up at the third floor and a window opens slowly, just go on and don't look back — especially if you know the place is locked up and no one living is inside. Otherwise, you might see someone staring at you with anger.

Update: I stopped by the Nelson House on Wednesday, May 19, 2010, after taking pictures of Grace Episcopal Church and its cemetery, and met a man trimming the trees on the property. He used to work as a janitor inside the house and told me that the place has a hidden staircase. He also never had any experiences in the house or anywhere else in his life.

THE MOORE HOUSE

The Moore House was the chosen site for negotiations when Cornwallis surrendered. During the siege, it was owned by Augustine Moore and his wife, Lucy. Located one mile east of Yorktown, it stands on one of the earliest patented lands in Virginia that is on a high plateau above the York River. It is a large, two-story place that is painted white, and has two brick chimneys at each end and a gambrel-style roof completing it. It survived the Revolutionary War, but a stray bullet shot and killed Augustine Moore Jr. while he worked the family fields.

One ghost story connected to the house concerns not the owners of the place, but another man, John Turner. He was killed by accident on October 13, 1781 when he was viewing the bombardment during the siege. They rushed him to nearby Moore House. His wife, Clara, was there to do what she could for her husband while they waited for a doctor. It didn't matter; he died. Whoever he was to Moore House or its residents at the time of his death, his grave is on the grounds. His tombstone had for a century been stored in the basement of the house, until finally it was put over what is believed to be his final resting place.

As for Clara, her death is blamed on pining away for her husband. It is her ghost that is thought to haunt Moore House and its grounds. Her face has been seen peering out of a second-story window. Other witnesses have seen her apparition standing at the edge of the York River. One resident of Yorktown saw her crying into a handkerchief and then dabbing at her eyes with it. He knew she was not of this world, when a light from a passing car passed through her and shone on the trees behind her.

The stories go that Augustine Moore also haunts Moore House. The sheets on the bed in the master bedroom have been found with indentations as if someone had been sleeping in it — and a depression in a red velvet chair was found in the parlor. Just as if someone had sat in it!

Those who claim to be psychic tell that they have sensed the presence of Augustine Moore, Jr. when they came to the house.

One witness, Patty Ceran, made two trips to this house. The first one was with her daughter and grandson. Her grandson said he saw a lady on the porch, standing by his mother when she posed for a photo. Patty also took a photo on the porch and she heard a noise.

I finally got to Moore House myself on May 21, 2010, to find men painting the outside and it closed. I snapped a couple shots of the front of the house and of the graveyard by the road on the lawn. Except for the workers, the place was quiet and peaceful. Nothing out of the ordinary happened to me that day.

No matter who really haunts the place, Moore House still has unseen people living in it!

Moore House.

John Turner's grave in the cemetery.

OTHER YORKTOWN HAUNTINGS

Crier Building

Where once a man named Nicholas lived, it is said that he now haunts a converted office building. He is buried in a grave on the front lawn, marked by his tombstone. Footsteps are heard, along with workers sensing his presence. This can make for unpleasant working conditions. The building is located downtown in Yorktown.

Scary Encounter in an Apartment

While living in Yorktown several years ago in the Chelsea Apartments, a young boy walked into the bathroom and came right back out. His mother told him to go right back in there and to use the restroom before he would be allowed to go to bed.

The boy said, "There's a man in there."

His mother knew there wasn't anyone in there because her husband, the boy and his brother, and she were the only ones there. She felt it had to be his imagination, so she told him to use the bathroom.

He yelled at her, saying that the man would get very mad. Determined to prove to him no man was in their bathroom, she took him into the bathroom. Like she thought, no one was in there.

After he used the bathroom, she had him sit down at the kitchen table with her and his father. The mother asked what this man looked like.

The boy said, "The man looked like one of those soldiers you see in one of those Civil War movies. He had red hair and wore a gray uniform."

His father remarked that it was a bunch of nonsense. Just then, the glass in the bottom of their entertainment center blew out. It was as if someone had shot at the glass, but it blew out, not in.

Another time the mother even noticed a balloon floating across the living room when there was absolutely no breeze there, or anyone else in the apartment but her.

Haunted Grace Church

Grace Church was built in 1697. The church is made of an oyster-shell substance called marl. Grace saw good fortune until Cornwallis and his army marched in Yorktown. They made the church into a storage facility for their gunpowder. They trashed the pews, windows, and furniture.

There are those who still believe that this desecration of the church caused the English to be defeated. They felt that divine intervention raised the waters when some of the English and Germans tried to escape across the York River.

It was in 1814 that a legend arose that another army of Englishmen came to Yorktown, angry over the defeat of the English in the War of 1812. They set the town ablaze and reduced the church to a blackened ruin. There is no proof that the English were behind this — just a statement that before the fire English ships were seen in Chesapeake Bay.

In the Civil War, the church once again was destroyed by a blast, and once again, it was rebuilt. It still serves as one of the main churches in Yorktown.

This church, though, also has ghosts. Colonial-era funerals with mourners have been seen in the cemetery surrounding the church. It would be alright if it was during the Colonial era — except the first recorded incident of this was in 1791 by Samuel Hawkins, who wrote about it in his journal, and it has been going on up to this day. A modern witness saw the funeral, and noted the women wore long black skirts to the ground and had hats that concealed their faces. The men were dressed in pants that ended at the knees, shoes with buckles, white stockings that stopped at the knees, and some wore capes. One of the phantom women actually fainted and was caught by one of the men.

Another apparition of a woman holding a dead infant has been sighted inside the actual church, kneeling at the back. She is sobbing. Then she vanishes.

I visited the church on May 19, 2010 and found people working inside and the cemetery peaceful as I photographed various graves. Nothing abnormal appeared in the photos and nothing in the EVP I recorded.

Grace Episcopal Church.

Grace Episcopal Church is located at 111 Church Street. The graveyard is open to anyone, and sometimes the church is open to visitors, too. For more information, the phone number is 758-898-3261; the website is www.gracechurchyorktown.org.

Scary Great Valley Road

Supposedly the most paranormal-active spot in Yorktown is Great Valley Road. In the 1700s this road wound down this ravine from "Maine Street" on the bluff to Water Street "under the hill," then a busy shorefront. Besides shipping out tobacco, legends say that they also would walk slaves up the trail as well as merchandise that came in on the cargo ships. Voices have been recorded here, as well as cold spots and mists that appear from nowhere. This is where some paranormal groups have investigated, capturing EVPs. I walked down this road to find Cornwallis' Cave in fall 2009. No EVPs captured and no odd feelings.

Surrender Road

There is a legend that if you drive down the road and see a little girl in a yellow dress, you are advised to turn around and go back, because "you will die."

The Revolutionary War Goes On

In a field across from the Nelson House, men in red coats have been spotted running around the property. Funny thing, this is nowadays, and there were no reenactments happening at the time. I checked the area out and found nothing. No EVPs recorded and no pictures either. I could find no other stories either, just the one.

Big Bethel Reservoir

In York County, Big Bethel Reservoir stands where a Revolutionary War and Civil War battlefield once was. Located on Big Bethel Road, it had served as the drinking water supply for Fort Monroe many years ago. The fort is now connected to Newport News Waterworks, so this water source is no longer necessary for that purpose — although it is still officially a part of Fort Monroe.

There have been many casualties there thanks to both wars. Some legends tell that it also had been sacred ground to the Pamunkey Indians before the Revolutionary War. Besides several drownings, some alleged kidnappings and rapes occurred there. One of the most famous deaths happened in 1988. This was the drowning of Dewy Banks, who fell out of a canoe. No one witnessed it, though they discovered his body several weeks later.

What has this got to do with ghost stories about the place? Strange occurrences have been reported over the years, like weird fog and balls of lightning. People have even claimed to hear their names called out. Is it all to do with these modern deaths, or from past battles? No one has answered that yet.

Most times it is said to be a great spot to go fishing, but beware if you do it very early in the morning or at night. For you just might catch more than fish for your dinner. Instead, you just might see things of a paranormal nature.

Chapter Four

JAMESTOWN ISLAND

"He that will not work shall not eat."
— Captain John Smith

Jamestown is where the first English colonists settled. Some of these were Captain John Smith, George Percy, and Gabriel Archer in 1607. They had been sent by the Virginia Company of London. The land must have seemed like paradise to these men and women when they came ashore, with forests of many different kinds of trees and rich land. They also came searching for gold and a route to the Orient. These intrepid explorers must have been happy to reach shore after leaving England during a gray, chilly winter and spending the next four and half months at sea, cramped aboard three ships that weren't big.

Spring had just come to Virginia when they arrived. Following orders given by the Virginia Company to settle inland about one hundred miles from the ocean, where a major river narrowed and offered defensive positions against enemies (Spanish), they sailed inland. An island was spied and they settled there. This is known as Jamestown Island today, off the Appomattox River. Another reason they chose this place: by order of the Virginia Company, they were not to upset any natives by taking over the land they already lived on. The island was vacant. On May 14, 1607, the 104 surviving colonists —all of them men — stepped foot on the land.

Of course, the Indians did come and eventually mounted an assault against the Englishmen. The colonists won the battle, but it taught them to fortify the fort for their own safety. Of course, some departed, and twenty-five of the men died by disease, wars, and for the most part from famine. It was Smith who later claimed sixty-five men actually died. More immigrants arrived, including some Germans and a Pole, along with the first two women, Mistress Forest and her maid, Anne Burras.

In the winter of 1609-10, starvation came and where there had been 215 colonists, only sixty survived. Of course, more arrived from England to settle the land. Although the suffering did not totally end at Jamestown for decades, some years of peace and prosperity followed the wedding of Pocahontas, the favored daughter of the Algonquian chief Powhatan, to tobacco entrepreneur John Rolfe at the Citie of Henricus. The Algonquians attacked the plantations that lay outside of Jamestown in 1624, killing over three hundred settlers.

The King revoked the Virginia Company Charter and Virginia became a crown colony. The capital moved to Williamsburg in 1698. The remains of Jamestown slowly began to disappear aboveground. During the American Revolution, a military post was put on the island. American and British prisoners were exchanged there. Confederate soldiers occupied it in 1861. They built an earth fort near the Jamestown church to block the Union's advance up the James River. Unfortunately, the only battle that happened was between two Confederate forces, as both troops thought they were fighting a Union army. After that, not much attention was paid to Jamestown until preservation was undertaken in the twentieth century. So, you can see why there are many reasons for hauntings on this island — there are stories of voices heard when no one was there and sometimes, a spectral figure is seen.

Statue of Captain John Smith on Jamestown Island.

Another reason the English came to the New World was the hope of converting the natives to Christianity. They must have thought that this wild land was filled with witches and demons. King James mentioned that demons roamed the wild areas of the world, and that the Devil lingered where the greatest ignorance and barbarity was a part of daily life. What did John Smith and the others think of the Native Americans as they watched them perform their tribal dances in painted faces?

Virginia must have been considered a battleground between forces of good and evil, as idols worshipped by the Indians were considered representations of the Devil. One of these idols, "Okee," was considered to be a "devil-witch" by John Smith himself. When one of the colonists, Alexander Whitaker, and others with him explored the Nansemond River, they came upon some Indians doing a dance. A native told them that it would rain shortly, so when a storm happened, Whitaker wrote, "All which things make me think that there be great witches amongst them and they (are) very familiar with the devil."

Some graves of settlers who died on Jamestown Island.

In fact, according to author and historian Richard Beale Davis, a conviction of witchcraft did result in the early days of Virginia. A witch was found guilty and executed on-board a ship bound for Jamestown. At that time, it was believed witches conjured up storms at sea and caused illness among the passengers, so when a severe storm struck, its captain ordered the death of a woman named Catherine Grady…all because she was a "witch at sea." Author Davis also pointed out ten years later, a letter in the English State papers wrote about "the anticipated loss of a British ship with all on-board, because two witches sat in the maintop and could not be dislodged."

Ambler Plantation House

A ghost story centers on what is left of Ambler Mansion. It is said that the spirit of Lydia Ambler haunts the ruins.

After the capitol moved from Jamestown to Williamsburg in the mid-1700s, two families bought and settled two separate areas of the 1,500-acre island. These were the Amblers and the Travises.

The Amblers built their home in Georgian style. They had a long boardwalk with flowers on each side of it as it led down to the river. Theirs was a lonely existence, particularly for the oldest daughter, Lydia, but not long after the Revolution began, it was whispered she met a young man, Alexander Maupin. He visited Jamestown, hoping to obtain financial support for the Patriots. Not long after his arrival, he married Lydia in August 1776.

Lydia wore a long, white-laced gown for the wedding, and she glided down the boardwalk, her train sweeping after her. She met Alexander at the end on the pier and married the young soldier there. Not long after, he received her large dowry and departed off to the war. Lydia believed he would return to her.

Day after day, she stood on the pier and watched for his return. Eventually, she grew angry, feeling that he had deserted her. She felt pretty certain that if he had fallen in battle, someone would have gotten word to her.

In 1781, something would happen to make her forget her errant husband for a while. Benedict Arnold and his force swept through the Virginia Peninsula, burning everything belonging to those who were suspected of being Patriot sympathizers. One of these places set ablaze was the Ambler home. No longer with a place to live, the family moved from relative to relative. When the war ended in 1781, the family rebuilt their home. Once again, Lydia could focus on Alexander. She kept watch for him, until she broke down and admitted that he married her for her dowry and would never be returning. Unable to take the truth, she took her own life.

The mansion burned again during the Civil War and once again, it was rebuilt, but when a fire happened for the third time to the place, it was abandoned. Nothing is left, but a memory of the glory in the ruins still standing and one Ambler that still haunts her old homestead.

There are those who claim to witness the phantom of Lydia there. One of them is a costumed interpreter for Jamestown. She saw Lydia walking one day. The interpreter had stayed late, giving a special tour to some French tourists. When everyone had gone, except for someone working in the bookstore, she went for a walk to smoke a cigarette. She sat on a bench at Ambler and admitted she felt some "presence." Deciding that maybe she should leave, that was when she saw a young woman in a gown from the eighteenth century come from around the back of the mansion to head down to the river. At first she thought her to be another employee — until she saw her floating in mid-air about two feet off the ground. The spirit turned around and sped toward the woman. She looked angry, too. The guide took off and didn't look back. When she did glance back, she saw that the woman had vanished.

You can tour this island and watch archeologists from Preservation Virginia digging down into where the fort is or walk the island and find the Ambler Mansion ruins. A fee is charged and the place is open every day (except Christmas) from 8:30 a.m. to dusk. Jamestown Island is at the end of Colonial Parkway and can also be reached by following Jamestown Road. For more information, check out Jamestown Island's website at http://www.nps.gov/jame/index.html.

If you are on the island at dusk just before it closes, don't get caught by the ruins of the Ambler Mansion. You just might be chased from them by one angry wraith.

Remains of the Ambler Plantation House.

NEITHER TREE NOR FAMILY CAN SEPARATE TRUE LOVE

"We loved with a love that was more than love."
— Edgar Allan Poe

There is a couple buried in the cemetery behind Jamestown Memorial Church. A legend that involves a sycamore tree says that it separates them in death, accomplishing supposedly what their families never could do in life.

In the 1700s, James Blair served as counsel to the British Government and became governor of the Virginia colony later on. He is considered the founder of the College of William and Mary in Williamsburg. All of this would make him a worthy suitor for any young woman. He was handsome, too. Any parent would be proud that he paid suit to their daughter, but Sarah Harrison's parents did not see it that way.

Age seventeen and the oldest daughter of Colonel Benjamin Harrison of Wakefield Plantation, Sarah was active in plantation social life. She was not only beautiful, but also a headstrong girl. Many eligible suitors paid court to her. Her parents approved of marriage to one of them, a young man named William Roscoe.

Except she met James Blair three weeks later, after her engagement had been announced. She fell in love with him and it seemed that he did likewise. A love affair deemed doomed from the start. Not only because of her engagement to Mr. Roscoe, but because James was twice her age. In those days, any girl who married an older man became a disgrace to her parents, since society viewed such marriages as a sign of the girl's family's failing finances.

The headstrong Sarah, though, did not stay away from James. Legend has it that her fiancé, William Roscoe, died of a broken heart after she broke their engagement. Not long after, she and James married. Her parents did not attend the wedding and would have nothing to do with the couple. They tried many things, from trying to get it annulled to even drawing up legal papers. During a trip to see an attorney about this, Colonel Harrison, his wife, and their youngest daughter were killed when lightning during a storm struck their carriage.

The Blairs went on to live happily as man and wife until Sarah passed away in 1713 at the age of forty-two. Never forgiven by her family, she could not gain entrance into the Harrison family plot and instead got buried in a stone crypt just outside it, in a small cemetery within grasping fingers' reach of the Jamestown Memorial Church on Jamestown Island.

James lived another thirty years. When he finally died in 1743, he was laid to rest in another stone crypt about six inches from his wife's tomb.

In 1750, a sycamore tree began to grow next to James's crypt, right between his tomb and his wife's. Nothing was done to prevent its growth and it grew and grew until it shattered the bricks between the two crypts. This caused Sarah's headstone to move into the nearby Harrison plot, only a short distance from her parents' and her sister's graves.

The story doesn't end there. Not long ago, the old sycamore tree, which had grown very large, had died and was cut down. The broken bricks and shattered tombs had been left as they were. Not long after another sycamore tree sprouted in the very same spot. By all appearances, it appeared that the Harrisons still worked from beyond the veil to keep their daughter from James.

James Blair's and Sarah Harrison Blair's graves.

Jamestown Memorial Church.

Just as it was so back on October 28, 2008, I found the two lovers' graves side-by-side, no sycamore tree separating them. All of the graves in that church cemetery were laid out in a row, no doubt put that way by the Association for the Preservation of Virginia Antiquities (APVA). I'm pretty sure that the preservation society dug out that tree long ago, but the romantic in me still believes that maybe James got his wish and the two of them are together in death just as they had been in life. Doesn't happily-ever-after always sound better with any story?

PHANTOM CAR AT WELLS'S CORNER

There's a more modern ghost story that a phantom car with a rumble seat has been seen near the intersections of County Roads 631 and 610 in James City County. A man dressed in a dark suit bends over the engine, apparently checking it over. He has been honked at by people in vehicles driving by, but he never looks up at them. Then, as they pass him, the man and his car disappear.

The legend goes on to say that a car struck him down in the 1930s while he worked on the engine. Is this a residual, or is this a ghost still determined to get his car running again? Or is it just an interesting urban legend? I've been to the area and did not have any run-in with this phantom.

Section Two

OTHER HAUNTS IN THE HISTORIC TRIANGLE AREA

Though the Triangle is mainly Williamsburg, James City County, and Yorktown, there are other counties and towns nearby in this portion of the Virginia Peninsula that have supernatural occurrences — and many of them have been well-known for years. It wouldn't be fair if I left them out of this book. After all, once you're checking out the Historic Triangle, why not mosey over to these nearby places?

Learn about the haunted plantations of Charles City, dance with the Devil, or join Jeb Stuart's ghost on a ride. Visit Gloucester's Rosewell where a spirit of a woman has been seen and maybe even heard.

Now go ahead and turn the page — if you dare!

Chapter Five

CHARLES CITY

Charles City, Virginia, lies between Williamsburg and Richmond. It adopted the slogan "Four Centuries, Three Cultures, Two Rivers in One County" as part of the commemoration of America's 400th Anniversary.

Algonquian-speaking Native Americans migrated to the area from up north about eight hundred years before the Jamestown Settlement. Before they came, other tribes had occupied it as early as 10,000 years before. Then the Europeans came in 1613 to start a settlement at West and Shirley Hundred.

Tobacco plantations grew and, during the late 1600s and early 1700s, the labor of enslaved Africans replaced the English indentured servants used at first. When the Civil War brought emancipation to the slaves, it forced residents to find other ways to earn their livelihood. Logging, fishing, and small-scale farming became the primary way of life for Charles City residents well into the 1900s. Not many residents in the area do this today though.

Since the first quarter of the eighteenth century, the county has comprised an area of 204 square miles bounded by the James River on the south, the Chickahominy River on the east and north, and Turkey Island Creek on the west. Charles City County has one of the oldest governmental units in America and was named after the son of King James who later became King Charles I of England. It was created by the Virginia Company in 1619.

Today the Native Americans are still in the area. The Chickahominy tribe is the second largest of eight Virginia Indian tribes. Its members are around eight hundred. Most of the tribe live on a high ridge in the vicinity of the river, with the Tribal Center and the adjoining Samaria Baptist Church being the heart of this community.

The tribe is headed by a chief and two assistant chiefs. Instead of taking these positions due to heredity, they are voted in by election. The Chickahominy Pow-Wow is held the last weekend in September and draws 3,000 to 5,000 visitors from all over the United States. Bill and I attended one of these a couple of years ago. Indians donned in traditional dress performed many of their dances.

Charles City has miles of forest, country stores, taverns, and homes. It also has many plantations, including Shirley, Berkeley, Edgewood, North Bend, Upper Weyanoke, and Kittiewan (which houses the Archeological Society of Virginia). Churches, like the historic Westover Parish, are there too, and there is the Virginia Capital Trail.

Now that you have learned about Charles City, flip to the next page to read what spirits haunt it.

Welcome to Charles City sign.

A Native American dancer at the Pow-Wow.

BERKELEY PLANTATION

"Great lives never go out; they go on." — Benjamin Harrison

Berkeley Plantation lies at Harrison's Landing on the James River on scenic Route 5, not far from Williamsburg and not even from Richmond. Part of a grant made in 1619 by King James I to the Berkley Company, designated it as "Berkley Hundred." A band of Indians stormed the settlement and killed nine people on Good Friday in 1622. It was abandoned some years later and not reclaimed until 1636. John Bland, a merchant from London, received the property. His son, Giles Bland, was a favored lieutenant of Nathaniel Bacon, a rebellion leader of Bacon's Rebellion. When Bacon's insurrection failed in 1676, Governor Sir William Berkley ordered Giles to be hanged. Berkley came into possession by Benjamin Harrison III and it was his son, Benjamin Harrison IV, who built the original Georgian mansion in 1726 out of brick fired on the plantation.

It is the birthplace of William Henry Harrison, the ninth president of the United States, along with Benjamin Harrison V, signer of the Declaration of Independence. It is also the ancestral home of Benjamin Harrison, our twenty-third president.

The mansion claims to be the oldest three-story brick house in Virginia, with proof of its date, and is the first with a pediment roof. It occupies a beautifully landscaped hilltop site overlooking the historic James River. The date of the building, plus the initials of the owners, Benjamin Harrison IV and his wife, Anne, appear in a date stone over a side door. The Adam woodwork and the double arches of the 'Great Rooms' were installed by Benjamin Harrison VI in 1790 at the direction of Thomas Jefferson.

Five terraced gardens sweep down from the house to the James River. All had been dug by hand before the Revolutionary War. On adjacent farmland, sheep graze on this almost 1000-acre plantation where miles of old fashioned gravel roads forge through it. Wildlife abounds in this delightful, peaceful setting. Anyone can linger at the river's edge and enjoy the gentle lapping water and soft river breezes when they take the tour of the house.

Berkeley Plantation House.

The Haunting

Is it haunted? That's what some of us with the Vasper Meetup group intended to find out a couple of years ago. Vasper was led by Beth Brown (author of *Haunted Plantations of Virginia* and *Haunted Battlefields of Virginia*), who set up a ghost tour of the mansion for us in October 2007 (the Vasper Meetup group no longer exists). My husband and I got there early to check the outside part of the place. When everyone had arrived, we were allowed in to take the tour of the house. I took lots of photographs and used my digital recorder. I got quite a few orbs and anomalies in some of the pictures. While I didn't get anything on my recorder, others had, like Jackie Tomlin, the head of the group I am with currently, Central Virginia Psychic Development and Paranormal Investigation. At the cemetery, I smelled the distinct odor of tobacco around me. No one was smoking in our group that night, especially not out there. Did that mean a spirit was hanging around me? Good question. However, there was no evidence other than what my own nose breathed in. Afterwards, we talked excitedly about experiences we had and then left to drive home. The night was nice and comfortable in temperature.

There have been stories about the place told over the years, way before we came. Some have been recorded by other authors, some told by those who experienced the phenomena. One of those tales concerns Benjamin Harrison IV. In 1744, when a bad thunderstorm hit the area, Benjamin Harrison IV dashed through the mansion, closing windows and locking shutters, but a particular window upstairs gave him trouble. He called for help and it arrived in two of his daughters, one carrying Benjamin's infant son, Benjamin Harrison V. Unfortunately, this story has a sort of sad ending, for a flash of lightning struck them and all were killed except the baby. There was a doctor there at the time as a dinner guest. He "bled" young Benjamin, who survived and grew up to become president of the American Colonies, signed the Declaration of Independence, married, and sired William Henry Harrison. William, or "Tippecanoe" as he was nicknamed, was elected to become the ninth president of the U.S., while his grandson, Benjamin Harrison, became the 23rd.

The story doesn't quite end there. It is said that Benjamin Harrison IV and at least one of the daughters are a couple of the phantoms that haunt the plantation. Many of the residents, staff members, and even visitors over the years have had encounters with them.

One of the common manifestations has to do with the balky bedroom window. Periodically, it slams shut by itself. This would be by the residents since visitors are not allowed to go up from the first floor.

Others talk about a young woman with a baby in her arms. She stands at the window late at night, but when someone gets to the spot, she is gone.

Orb in road nearby the Berkeley Plantation family cemetery.

Freaky Experiences

A photographer visited the plantation once to take some photographs of the place. One he took in the south parlor happened to be of the portrait of Mrs. Jamieson's great grandmother, Elizabeth Burford. After he developed the film, he found a picture of another person entirely. He thought that the staff moved the portraits, but no one had. He rented a television camera and set it up in the house to shoot for a proposed documentary, but the camera wouldn't work. He thought something was wrong with it; except when he got it back to the camera shop, it worked with no problem.

Tour guide, Vickey Hoover, had a number of things happen to her. In her opinion, she feels it is Benjamin Harrison himself. When she joined the staff, she didn't believe in ghosts. The ones at Berkeley made her a believer very quickly.

Vickey said that most likely Benjamin thought she was being disrespectful. Standing in the front hall beside the linen press, the door swung open and smacked her on the shoulder. It happened to her three or four more times. When she explained the phenomenon to some tourists one day, the door swung open, and she had to show them that she hadn't pressed any secret lever to make it open. Another time she had returned from maternity leave and made a joke that Benjamin must not have known she was back. At that moment, three knocks sounded. When she turned around to look, the door swung open.

Both Vickey and another tour guide have heard rattling from time to time. The door rattled when she was in the laundry room alone, and she also heard a baby's cry coming from the basement. Nothing was down there. When she went back upstairs to the breakfast room, the crying stopped.

One weird phenomenon that occurs is when someone passes the candelabra — the glass in it tinkles.

Large orb indoors the Berkeley Plantation House.

Another time Mrs. Jamieson called over to the tour guides in the adjacent building from the main house, demanding to know who was in her attic. She was adamant about the footsteps she heard from up there. One of the guides checked out the attic, but found the door bolted shut as it always is. She even went outside to see if any workmen had a ladder propped up against the building and were working around the attic, but again, nothing.

Many manifestations happen in the Berkley dining room. Tourists claim that they feel a presence the minute they walk into the room. Most of the phenomena center on a fruit bowl on the dining room table. One of the tour guides, Virginia Anders, put an apple in the bowl and before she even left the room, heard it drop. To her surprise, as she turned around, she saw the apple floating through the air and go over a Chinese screen. She bolted from the room. Others have seen apples come out and fall to the floor. One time, a lemon, fixed to a nail in the bowl, seemed to manage to get free, pop out, and roll across the table. When this fruit phenomenon happens, it is usually in the wintertime, around January, February, and March.

Another time, just before the first tour of the morning, a guide, Jan Wycoff, found peanuts scattered across the table. Wondering where they came from, she asked Vickey Hoover about them. She asked if Vickey would clean it up. Vickey never found any peanuts in the room. They had vanished.

Not all ghost stories centering on Berkeley are real. Take the legend of a ghost in a dip in the road that leads to the mansion. The legend goes to say that it is haunted by a young child who cries at night. Some discounted it, claiming that it is only an owl. It is believed that plantation owners encouraged the tale to keep slaves in their quarters at night. The owners felt this kept the slaves fresh for working in the morning and thought the ghost tale did more good than harm.

The Author's Experience

I've been back to the Berkeley Plantation, this time to take a regular house tour on Friday, April 30, 2010. My recorder had gotten stuck and wouldn't shut off, but worked fine later. I couldn't say that was due to any supernatural influences. I caught nothing on my EVPs, just birds. In one photo, though, the one of the Berkeley gift shop, I saw something odd in the top right-hand window. When I drew the photo on my computer closer to that window, I think I caught a face and kind of figure! Not a living person, as this seems white and phantom-like. It looks like a woman, even though this place was used for the young men and boys of the family in its past.

Berkeley is open daily, 9 a.m. to 5 p.m. It's only closed on Thanksgiving and Christmas. To find out more, check the website at www.berkeleyplantation.com. When you take the tour and you happen to see fruit leap out of a bowl, off the table, and roll away, just ignore it. It's just one of the specters at Berkeley amusing themselves.

Berkeley Gift Shop.

Berkeley family cemetery
during the daytime.

SHIRLEY PLANTATION

The Shirley Plantation is off of the John Tyler Memorial Highway. It can be found by either I-295, or turning left off Old Hundred Road onto Jordan Point Road /VA-106 N/VA-156 N and traveling over the Benjamin Harrison Bridge into Charles City County. You'll see a sign to your left, telling you how to get to Shirley from there.

Eleven generations of the same family owned and worked the land since 1613, when it became Virginia's first plantation. Just six years after the Jamestown Settlement was established, the crown grant enabled Shirley Plantation to become a reality. Work began on the mansion in 1723 when Elizabeth Hill, great-granddaughter of the first Hill, married John Carter, eldest son of Robert "King" Carter. It was completed in 1738, and referred to as the "Great House." In the late 1700s, Charles Carter placed the wooden pineapple at the peak of the roofline. This is a universal sign of southern hospitality, welcoming river travelers to Shirley.

This is where Robert E. Lee's mother, Ann Hill-Carter, married his father, Henry Lee III, at the time governor of Virginia and a member of Congress. Lee's skilled horsemanship had earned him the nickname "Lighthorse Harry" and he was esteemed for his combat heroics in the Revolutionary War where he served under General George Washington.

There is only 750 acres left of what had been 4,000 acres. Today, it is still a working farm, with soybeans, cotton, corn and wheat planted. Most of this is leased out to local farmers in the area. The place is a National Historic Landmark. The entire property and the house are under conservation easements protecting them from development. Before they can even work on some part of the house, making any changes, they must go through the Virginia Historical Resources. If any digging on the land is attempted, an archeological team must be there to do it first and even afterwards, an archeologist must be there to supervise any regular digging, just in case. All this is because the family motto today is "To preserve the past." Since the land can't be used just in any way to make money, the family has allowed polo matches, clay shooting, and even tried weddings (though this hasn't worked well).

As I found out, one cabin of the slave quarters is still standing, but not on Shirley land. The younger son, who inherited that parcel of land, sold off the land along with the cabin. Though Shirley has tried to purchase it back, even offering to keep someone on staff there, the current owners of the land haven't broken down. Hopefully, one day they will. The slave quarters were in three separate directions — mainly near the fields. All others but the one not on their land no longer is there for tourists to see. Another reason for all this needed protection of the land and the house is when they allowed sand and gravel mining. Due to this, the original stables were destroyed.

It was October 2009 when I rolled down the dirt road leading to Shirley. It was a nice fall day, comfortable to walk outside without getting overheated. I met with Julian Charity, Shirley's Visitor Service Supervisor, who took me on a tour of the house and the nearby buildings, since the director, Janet L. Appel, was away with one of the three plantation cats, Priscilla, who had to be put to sleep. I never got to see the other two cats, Tunnah and Sugah. I did get to meet her, though, as Ms. Appel came back before I took off on my own to explore the outer buildings. I also met the owner, Randy Carter, a very nice gentleman.

Besides the cats, there are nine goats led by Charlie (the only male in the herd) and a rooster, Kabob, with his hens. There hadn't been horses on the land (other than maybe a farmer's leasing some of the land from Shirley) since after the Civil War. Since the equines were status symbols anyway and the best had been taken by Northern troops, it was deemed better not to have them. They had kept hogs, but not since the 1980s and stopped keeping cattle by the 1950s. The family is attached to their animals, as they also have a pet cemetery in addition to the family one.

Shirley Plantation House.

Before they built and moved into the "Great House," they lived in Hill House. Saddest thing I heard was Edward Hill IV, the only son, died young from tuberculosis in 1702 before he could move with the family into Shirley. This also meant he never got to inherit the plantation when his father, Edward III, passed away. An interesting fact is that Edward III commissioned a memorial portrait done of his son. The artist never saw the boy. He painted Edward wearing a toga and sandals, sitting on his coffin, leaning against a tomb. He is pointing to a dark horse, which symbolizes death. This portrait hangs on the wall in the hallway of the front area of the house. Edward's death no doubt began the practice of having more than four children — and why men would remarry after appropriate mourning time, to have as many children as they could. One owner, Charles Carter (1777-1806), had twenty-three children, but only thirteen survived to make it into his will.

No doubt then, as he did with his later wife, Edward III did not eat meat while in mourning. This was a common practice at the time. When one's wife passed away in those days, they usually waited for three or four months before remarrying — a long time to go without meat! As for Edward III himself, he died in 1726. Besides Edward and Elizabeth, he had two older daughters, Martha (Aunt Pratt) and Hannah. Both married men in England and lived there, which is why neither got the house.

Another fascinating true story happened during the Civil War. The seventh generation wife of Randolph Carter contracted pneumonia a year after she buried her son, when she went to the family cemetery to mourn him. The family couldn't bury her during the day, due to attracting attention from Northern soldiers, and the servants would not help bury her at night due to superstition. The family had to do it all alone at night, by lantern light.

While it never went out of the family's hands, the Shirley Plantation survived the Indian Uprising, Bacon's Rebellion, the Revolutionary War, the Civil War, and the Great Depression.

Visitors that tour the house can see features such as the "Flying Staircase" and the Queen Anne Forecourt, plus other furnishings. The house is surrounded by several support buildings, including a two-story kitchen with living quarters, a two-story laundry with living quarters,

Aunt Pratt's Portrait. *Courtesy of the Shirley Plantation.*

a smokehouse, a stable building, an ice house, a large storehouse, and a dovecote. Besides being privately owned, it needs no assistance from any foundations or government agencies. The revenue from admission fees support preservation of this place.

Photography is not allowed inside the house (due to historical value of original furnishings and paintings on walls). Even I was not allowed to take pictures inside, but Shirley gave me a photo of Aunt Pratt's portrait from them to be used with permission.

Many of the furnishings and pieces in the house are original. The oldest is from the 1700s: a breakfast table that was in the kitchen before it was brought into the house in the 1980s.

In what is now the sitting room was where the parents ate at most of the time while the kids, until they were considered old enough (13 or 14 years old), ate elsewhere. It could also function for small dinners and the family used it for guitar and violin lessons, even piano. When expanded, and with the backdrop of the James River, the room was used for parties and large dinners. It was not as big as the ballrooms in many of other plantations though; the family was more concerned with the ornamental woodwork than an expansive room. Dancing could take place, as musicians played on the staircase while people danced in the combined rooms. One of the popular dances was the Virginia reel.

There is the original silverware and flatware that is not on view for visitors. It survived the Civil War as the family buried it on the property instead of storing it in the vaults in Richmond. Lucky for them, as the vaults were set on fire and everything in them burned.

Yes, with a long history and being a plantation, it did have slaves. First recorded fact of this is 1616: twenty-five white indentured servants were seen planting and curing tobacco. Indentured servants were of many different races and came from many different countries — Africa, the Caribbean Islands, Scotland, Ireland, and England; they were contracted to become laborers for a specified period of time in exchange for debt repayment, food, lodging, transportation to the colonies, and the teaching of a trade. In Virginia, since it was primarily agriculture, indentured servants became field hands and tended the tobacco fields. Africans first arrived in Virginia in 1619 and the first documented case of an African slave in Virginia was in 1640.

Besides the fields, slaves on Shirley tended the kitchen, which was outside, laundry, and the Great House. Most of the slaves lived in slave quarters, but those who worked the laundry lived upstairs in that building and those who served in the house lived upstairs there. I assumed those who cooked in the kitchen lived in the Great House too. Today the laundry building is used for the gift shop and the kitchen, which was in use until 1940, houses an exhibit.

More and more is being learned about slaves on Shirley. A new slavery exhibit was scheduled for completion in the latter part of 2010. It will be housed in the courtyard Kitchen building.

Shirley is also a wonderful spot to do bird-watching. They try to do couple of walks a year. One was just done in October before I came actually. That day I stood outside and looked up into the sky and saw an eagle soaring above the house. I thought it was a hawk, but Julian Charity told me he was pretty sure it was an immature eagle instead. There are many places along the place to sit and picnic and just watch all of the birds or just stare at the river drift by and enjoy the day.

The Haunting

Now for the ghost stories. There is the main one about "Aunt Pratt." No one is sure who called Martha Hill Aunt Pratt, whether it was Elizabeth's children or children's children, but that is what she is known by. Martha was taken to England where she met and married Hugh Gifford. She stayed there with him and never came back, dying in England. Her mother also passed away while in England, too.

Martha's portrait had been in the Hill House. Later, after Elizabeth moved into Shirley with John, her portrait, her mother's, father's and brother's came over to hang on the walls in the place. Years later, visitors admitted to being creeped out by the portrait and it was removed to the attic. That was when the ghostly occurrences began.

It appeared that Aunt Pratt did not care for being in the attic. And she let them know. Moans and groans, along with banging came from up there. She was brought down and hung on a wall inside a closet on the third floor. Again, she showed her displeasure by moans, groans and banging all night long. She was taken out of the closet and hung on a wall on the second floor. She was facing a window where Mrs. Carter thought she would enjoy the outdoor scenery. No, she did not. She moaned and groaned and banged so loud on the wall, that finally the portrait fell to the floor and cracked the frame (still broken today). They sent the portrait to a studio in Richmond to get the frame repaired. It was sent right back the next day, not touched at all. They complained of hearing moans, groans and banging.

Outdoor kitchen at Shirley Plantation where the ghost of a slave girl was seen.

Finally Mr. Carter took her to the master bedchamber on the first floor which served also as a study, library and private office. He hung her where the portrait is today and nevermore did they hear a peep from her.

They did test her one more time though. Shirley sent the portrait to New York City in the seventies, to a paranormal exhibit at Rockefeller Center. She let them know she was upset at this. She was always found on the floor, face down, by the watchman who knew she was on the wall when he locked up the place.

Another spirit seen at Shirley was a young boy about six or seven dressed in a gray suit. Visitors on in the long hallway saw him walking with them. No one knew who he was and by description, looked like his suit was from the nineteenth century.

I asked Julian if he had ever seen anything out of the ordinary. He hadn't, but he said there have been reports that the light of a small lamp in the bedchamber will go out. Also there are other stories of doors opening for no reason and sounds of someone creeping in the house. This always happen when someone's cell phone goes off or other things like that. Visitors admit to feeling cold chills come over them and one lady told Shirley that Aunt Pratt had spoken to her.

There is another ghost, one who haunts the kitchen. A young gentleman felt an energy presence around the doorway of the building and he saw a little slave girl standing there, looking at him. He told this to a worker in the gift shop afterwards.

Whether for the phantoms or the history itself, I greatly endorse a visit to this plantation. It is open seven days a week and is closed only on Thanksgiving and Christmas. To learn more, go to their website at www.shirleyplantation.com. One of their great events is the ghost walk to the family cemetery on Halloween, a place that normally tourists aren't allowed the rest of the year. The walk is led by the family ghost, "Aunt Pratt," and included in the price of admission, so you can come early to tour the house beforehand.

When you do visit and are in the room where Aunt Pratt's portrait is, don't be surprised if you think she speaks to you. History lives on here in more ways than one, even by supernatural means.

SHERWOOD FOREST

Sherwood Forest is also the home of President John Tyler from 1842 until his death in 1862. Sherwood Forest Plantation has been the residence of the Tyler family since the President purchased it in 1842. It is also known to be the longest frame house in America, over 300 feet long. The house expanded to its present length in 1845 when Tyler added a 68-foot ballroom to it. Today it is a National Historic Landmark, a Virginia Historic Landmark, and on the National Register of Historic Places. Sherwood is famous for having the ginkgo tree, the oldest one in America. It was given to President Tyler by Captain Matthew Perry when he returned from the Orient in the 1850s.

John Tyler was the tenth president of the United States, taking the position one month later after the inauguration of President Harrison, who died of pneumonia on April 4, 1841. Tyler served from 1841-1845. There's a myth told that he was never President. This could be attributed to the fact that he was the first vice president to take over for a president who died in office. The Constitution was vague about what to call such a chief executive, but the debate got settled and they called him "president." Still, there were those troublemakers citing contemporary news stories of the time. These stories referred to him as "Acting President," or even "His Accidency."

The grounds consist of twenty-five acres, including terraced gardens and a lawn based on the landscape designs of Andrew Jackson Downing of New York. This included original outbuildings or dependencies. It's considered one of the most complete plantation yards today.

It is also famous for its ghost. It boasts of the "Gray Lady," who has been heard rocking in the Gray Room since late in the eighteenth century, long before President Tyler bought it and moved in.

It is assumed she was a servant, maybe a nanny or governess, since she is seen wearing gray and gray was the color servants wore. The story goes that she would take the child from a first floor bedroom (which is now known, appropriately, as the Gray Room) and walk her up through the hidden staircase to a second floor nursery, where she would rock the child on her lap while rocking in a rocking chair, but the child grew ill and died. There are those who thought maybe she hadn't been attentive enough or not close to the child when it died, which makes it a possibly good enough "haunting" reason to still be hanging around. Whatever the reason, it is always the same: footsteps are heard going up or down the hidden stairway and then the rocking chair is heard in the second floor nursery and in the Gray Room… *rock, rock, rock.*

One of the Tylers, Payne, has heard it. Other people have, too. Usually when Payne Tyler heard the noise, it is always during the wee hours of the morning. Her husband, Harrison Tyler, scoffed at her at first — until it happened to him one night. He saw or heard her as she walked through his bedroom.

Another witness was a sixteen-year-old girl, who heard the ghost walking. She shrieked, freaking out. Another time it happened to a gardener. Payne was working in the yard and asked him to hand her a trowel a few feet away. He refused to go get it. What he did instead was walk all around the house. Payne scolded him about how long it took him. The man just stammered away, saying that he didn't want to walk past a door he saw opening and closing by itself. After that, he left the Tylers' employ.

Payne decided she would talk to the ghost. She told her that the Tylers had owned the place since the 1840s and they had a right to live in it. If she wanted to stay there, then both the living and the dead would have to peacefully coexist. Seems it worked.

Well, almost. A cousin of Harrison's paid a visit. She laughed and chided Payne when Payne told her about her talk with the phantom. They were in the Gray Room at the time — that's when it struck. The room began to shake. Loud bangs like shutters slamming against the house echoed in the air. The cousin fled the house and didn't come back to visit for three or four years. With her no longer in the house, the vibrations and the sounds halted as if they never happened.

Two psychic experts visited the house on separate occasions to give Payne their impressions. One saw a "tiny woman in an off-color dress with an apron and black shoes" standing at the top of the stairs on the second floor. It was not an apparition, though, but someone real. The woman vanished as the psychic climbed up the stairs.

Sherwood Plantation House.

This is the oldest
ginkgo tree in the
United States.

The other psychic reported the same phenomena…except the psychic climbed the stairs and followed the woman into a bedroom. She saw her at an Empire wardrobe, sorting clothes. She described the wardrobe as dark brown, with a wide flange at the center, a large brass strip, and having the design of dolphins at each foot. This stunned Payne as Julia Tyler loved dolphins and it had been removed some years before. It had never been photographed and never mentioned in any literature about the house. There was no way that the psychic knew about it, or even what it looked like.

Instead of one, there are two ghosts in the house. Or are they residuals of those who lived there before, going about their daily lives?

I took a tour of the grounds myself on a Sunday. There was a couple doing it also, but we didn't interact. Sliding my money into the box, I grabbed a map and slipped onto the property.

I took pictures and did a recording. Found the famous ginkgo tree in the back of the house. Alone back there, it felt as if something watched me. I didn't think anyone was home. The place seemed quiet and deserted that day.

Sherwood Forest is located eighteen miles west of Williamsburg and thirty-five miles east of Richmond on Virginia Route 5. Its address is 14501 John Tyler Memorial Highway. It is open to do a self-guided tour of the grounds for a small fee, from 9 a.m. to 5 p.m. daily. To tour the house, you must set up an appointment. You can learn more by checking their website at http://www.sherwoodforest.org/index.html.

North Bend Plantation

Built in 1801 by John Minge in historic Charles City County for his wife Sarah Harrison, North Bend Plantation became the home of the sister of William Henry Harrison, ninth president of the United States. The current owner, George F. Copland, is a descendant of the brother and sister.

Thirty thousand Federal troops camped in 1861 in the area of North Bend. This caused Thomas Wilcox, the owner at that time, to leave for Belle Air Plantation. He never returned. Union General Phillip Sheridan headquartered at North Bend while his troops built a pontoon bridge across the James River. The desk used by the general is still at North Bend today.

North Bend Plantation is the best preserved of the academic Greek Revival Style buildings in Charles City County. It is a Virginia Historic Landmark and is also on the National Register. There are antiques, rare books, and old dolls within the walls, along with spacious bed chambers with canopy beds, antiques, and private baths. The house is surrounded by fields and countryside.

Besides all the luxurious furnishings and a place for a night of rest, there are the unseen residents of the place. Mrs. Copland herself experienced the paranormal. She woke up to pacing in her bedroom. Alone and concerned that it may be a burglar, she made a call to her son. When the sound of a car approaching reached her ears, the footsteps quit. Mrs. Copland and her son checked the whole building over but found nothing. When he left, the footsteps started up again. She called her son and he came over again, this time staying the night. He thought it was most likely the spirit of General Sheridan. Guests who have stayed at the bed and breakfast have also heard similar noises.

An interesting fact is about an antique at North Bend — an oriental porcelain Foo Dog dating from 1801. It is supposed to ward off evil spirits. With all goings on with the ghost, the dog isn't doing what it is supposed to do.

For more information about North Bend, visit their website at www. northbendplantation.com.

North Bend Plantation Bed and Breakfast.

EDGEWOOD PLANTATION

The legend goes that her lover, who was a Carter from Shirley Plantation, went away to fight in the Civil War and never returned. That she died from a broken heart, and her spirit waits for him, watching from her upstairs window. Guests have reported seeing the face of Lizzie Rowland looking out of an upstairs window at Edgewood Plantation. In the "Lizzie" Room at Edgewood her name is scratched on the window pane that she did herself.

Edgewood is a historic landmark circa 1849. Situated along Route 5, the house's third floor was used during the Civil War as a lookout post for Confederate generals to peer on the Northern troops when they were at nearby Berkeley Plantation. Besides the house and the grounds, there is the 1725 Benjamin Harris Grist Mill, which ground corn for both the Union and Confederate armies. Confederate General J.E.B. Stuart made his last stop at Edgewood on his way to Richmond to warn General Robert E. Lee of how much power the Union Army on June 15, 1862.

Edgewood had been part of the Berkeley Plantation once. Benjamin Harrison had gone to King Carter of Shirley and asked if he could purchase some land for a mill. He ended up buying 22,000 acres. In 1725, he built the grist mill. It was so successful that he built Berkeley Plantation in 1726. During the Revolutionary War, Benedict Arnold also visited here.

In 1840, maybe due to need for money, 1,800 acres and the mill were sold to a Yankee from New Jersey, Spencer Rowland. All was so well that Spencer built the house. He moved into it with his wife and daughter, Elizabeth (who was known more as Lizzie).

The Civil War broke out and though a Yankee, Spencer was accepted because he attended Westover Church, put much into the community and had the mill. The mill provided ground corn for both Confederates and the Union Army. When McClelland said he would stable his horses at Westover Church, Rowland became upset and offered Edgewood for church services. It was used for church services after the war for a while, too, as Westover was in bad shape.

In the early 1900s, Edgewood became Charles City County's first restaurant, the Blue Tea Pot. It was also the first telephone exchange in Charles City — a big party line. The current owners, Julian and Dot Boulware still have the one page telephone book for that exchange. Edgewood had also been used as a post office, too. Currently, it rents rooms as a bed & breakfast, offers Victorian high teas, and special themed tours.

It was September 19, 2009 that I drove to Charles City and Edgewood to talk to Dot about her bed and breakfast and its ghost. A nice sunny day, the weather seemed cooler and less muggy, an indication to me that fall was on its way. I found the place and turned into its driveway.

Making sure I had everything I needed, I got out of my car and walked up to the front porch. I knocked. The person who let me in was Dot's daughter-in-law, Candy. Seated in the living room, Candy and I talked about a couple of experiences she had with Lizzie.

The first time she heard Lizzie was in 1996. She was upstairs, cleaning the rooms, when she heard a knock on the door from downstairs. She rushed down the stairs to grab the door and open it. There was no one there. Candy went back upstairs to continue what she'd been doing. Not long after, another knock. And once again, she went downstairs and this time checked the back door. Still nobody. So she walked back up the steps. When a third knock came, Candy said, "Lizzie, I know it's you, and I am not coming downstairs again. You're not getting me for the third time."

Edgewood Plantation
Bed and Breakfast.

After that, no more knocks.

She saw Lizzie for the first time three years before the date of my interview. She had a Pampered Chef party. One of the guests had brought her three children. Being naughty that day, the kids ran up and down the staircase and jumped on the beds. Her mother-in-law, Dot, told her to get them off the beds and she got everyone downstairs to the kitchen. That was when she saw her, on the steps outside on the porch. What struck her as odd at the time was the phantom wore a mop cap. She froze. Suddenly, the ghost dissipated.

Dot came into the living room and introduced herself. A charming lady, she offered me something to drink and we began our interview about the history and ghost stories of Edgewood.

Her husband, Julian, and she were looking to buy an old house. They collected antiques and wanted a house for them and their sons. In 1978, a real estate agent said he had this place for them to look at. It was for sale at $150,000 (at that time it was like a million dollars). They wanted to see the land first, but the agent pressed on them to check out the house first.

The house was visible from the road and Dot's first thought had been: This can't be it? This place is $150,000? When they stepped inside, they found the paint chipping, a bulb hanging; in fact, it was in really bad shape. Dot saw a light coming down the stairs from upstairs when she had the thought that no one lived in the house. She looked up and saw the staircase for the first time.

It was really gorgeous, and she screamed in excitement.

They found a young girl in the place. The first thing she said when she saw them was, "It's haunted."

"What did you say?" Julian asked.

"It's haunted, sir."

That shocked Dot, as here was this place they were trying to sell and the first thing said is that it was haunted. Not a good way to sell something.

The girl got out a book, *Virginia Ghosts* by Marguerite DuPont Lee, and read the part about Edgewood Plantation.

As Julian was pulling Dot away and they were at the front door, Dot screamed, "Have you ever seen her?"

The girl replied, "We heard her."

Julian told her that to buy the place cost $150,000 and it would be another $150,000 to fix the place up. They couldn't afford that at all. Dot asked if they couldn't negotiate, but he answered, "How can you negotiate?"

Later, after he went on a business trip, Dot came back to see the house one more time. The owner himself was there and asked her why she was here.

"I want to see the staircase one last time."

He let her and then she turned to him. She told him they couldn't buy the place, even though she wanted to. After a bit, he lowered the selling price to $75,000. Dot took it. As Dot told me, she probably could have gotten him to lower it even more. He had it for sale for three years and she doubted he had one bite. Still, $75,000 was good. The house had that great staircase along with eight fireplaces. Though the grist mill no longer had its wheel (that was given to the WWII effort as scrap metal), they had that, too.

It took them a while to fix it up. Julian came when he got off work, which was at 3 p.m. Dot helped on the weekends, as she had the four boys. They had put in two gazebos and a pool, and then worked on the inside of the house.

It was when Julian came after work one night he had a run-in with the ghost. Usually he had a helper, Charles, but Charles had to work late and Julian felt uneasy being by himself. He heard something — and felt something around him. He sat down on a sawhorse.

"Lizzie, is that you? I want to tell you something. We're trying to make this place look nice. We've taken every piece of money to buy it and it will take a lot more to fix it up — and if you bother my family, I'll burn it to the ground!"

She did not bother him after that.

Dot admitted that Lizzie tested them when they first moved in, doing little things like turning lights on and off. One of their helpers, Jimmy, left with them and he knew the lights were all turned off. When he looked back at the house, though, all the lights were back on.

Slowly, Dot began to find out about the place. The house was older than she thought and of historical value. On April 9, 1979 there came a knock at the front door. She threw it open and found two young men in Confederate uniforms standing on the porch. Two horses were tied to the post at the house.

One of them spoke. "Are you Mrs. Rowland?"

Dot laughed. "The Rowlands? They lived in the 1800s and this is 1979!"

"I'm Jeb Stuart and this is my rider."

"Oh, really? Then I'm Florence Nightingale."

He looked at her. "No, we're two students from the College of William and Mary and what we're doing is a thesis on Jeb Stuart's ride. This was his last stop before he went to Richmond to warn General Robert E. Lee how much power the Yankees had."

They left after that.

Julian and she went to the Library of Virginia to learn more about their house. They learned about Benedict Arnold camping there. They learned that Benjamin Harrison bequeathed the mill to his wife so that when he passed away it would keep her in business. Edgewood wasn't just a house — it was history.

Lizzie Makes Herself Known

Besides the history, though, Edgewood had its haunt. Dot invited some friends over for hors d'oeuvres and drinks December 15, 1978. Ten couples in all, the men spent the time in the kitchen while the women were in the dining room. One friend asked Dot how she liked living in Charles City (she lived in Richmond before).

Another friend piped up, "We want to hear all about Lizzie."

That was when another of the women, Joyce Parker, broke in.

"I don't believe you all. There are no such things as ghosts. I don't believe in ghosts at all."

That's when a brass plate in a plate holder on the cupboard behind her flew over and struck her on the shoulder. Everyone was in shock. They all got up; Joyce went to the bathroom and the other girls grabbed their husbands and left.

One night in 1979, when they had lost electricity and she didn't leave the kerosene lamps on so as not to cause a fire, both Julian and she were awakened by someone coming up the steps. Now, I've been up and down those steps myself and they are loud. Dot is right in saying that if it was one of her sons sneaking in there was no way they could get away with it.

Julian grabbed a gun, which shocked her. "It's probably Lizzie," she said.

From where the plate flew off and hit Joyce Parker.

She rose from the bed and went to the door, opened it, but stayed at the threshold. She called out the names of the boys. No one answered her.

Julian stood behind her, gun in hand. He told her to go first and that he'd shield her. They both went downstairs, but found nothing.

One day, a woman dropped by with her daughter, Renee. Dot showed her the staircase and asked wouldn't it be grand for a bride to come down. Dot knew since she had only boys it would never happen for her. Two weeks later, she got a call. Seems the daughter got engaged and thought that it would be wonderful if her fiancée saw her coming down the stairs on their wedding day. Dot was nervous, as she'd never done a wedding before, but the day of the event, which had seventy-five guests, went off without a hitch. The bride and groom rode off in a carriage pulled by horses to the reception held at Berkeley.

A month later Renee called her. "Mrs. Boulware, guess who came to the wedding?"

Now, Dot worried. She had locked the third floor basement and the upstairs rooms since there was no reason for anyone to be in those places, so she couldn't think who.

"Lizzie!"

"Lizzie, who?"

"Your Lizzie. She's in a photo of the third floor window!"

Dot brought me the picture to show me. I saw something like a face peering from the window. Since she couldn't have her own wedding, it was as if she came to one that was held there. Did she watch while the bride tripped down the stairs to her waiting groom, something she never got to do?

Another picture she found from the 1970s had a face peering out of what is called Sara's room. There was no one in the room at the time. Was this Lizzie, or someone else?

Another couple, one in their 40s, married at Edgewood in a quiet ceremony. Afterwards, they had champagne and then left for Indian Fields Tavern to have their wedding dinner. Dot went upstairs to Lizzie's room, where they would stay for their wedding night, to turn down the bed. She found an old sword lying across the foot of the bed. She removed it long enough to turn down the bed and replaced it where it had been, then left the room. The man and his new wife had their portrait taken with the sword. The sword had been his gift to her, with an inscription etched on it.

The next morning, the couple came down to breakfast. Dot was there, having coffee with the guests.

"I hope everything went well," Dot said.

The woman looked to her husband and said, "Tell her."

The man blurted out. "I've experienced Lizzie!"

After the wedding, they went upstairs to change and the groom was having a hard time with the buttons on his shirt. Suddenly, he felt the light touch of someone on his shoulder. He thought it was his wife and called out. His wife answered from the bathroom. Cold chills overcame him. He knew who had touched him then.

His wife mentioned that when she came out of the bathroom, she found him standing there, white as a sheet.

Dot shared her belief as to why Lizzie made herself known to him particularly. "It's because you're an old soul and Lizzie can relate to that."

Other Edgewood Ghosts

Dot became friends with a historian, Nancy Carter. She was married to a Carter for forty-some years and was very factual. She was not someone given to flights of fancy. It was she who gave Dot a lot of information on Edgewood.

When she asked what she could do to help Dot as she was going out, Dot asked if she could turn down the beds upstairs. While Nancy was doing that, she heard someone coming up the steps. It sounded like the rustle of petticoats. She checked the hall, but found no one. Then Nancy rushed downstairs, but found no one on the steps or downstairs anywhere.

A lady and her husband stayed in Jeb Stuart's room one time. The next morning, she asked to speak to Dot. It seemed that she woke up in the middle of the night to the sound of petticoats rustling. She tried to get her husband to wake up, but he never did. So she sat up and looked to see who it was, except there was no one in the room with them.

Five years ago, a young man stayed at the bed and breakfast. When he came down to the dining room and had a cup of coffee, he said, "You have a man here. He visited me last night. I was lying in bed, my back to the fireplace and facing the window, when I rolled over. A man with old fashioned clothing and suspenders was next to me. I asked him if he needed anything and he answered, 'No, not right now.' I rolled back over and went to sleep."

Two women came to Edgewood. Both were into the ghost stuff. Dot read them the story from *Virginia Ghosts*. They said they wanted to stay the night and even visit Lizzie's grave at Westover Church cemetery. Dot told them they couldn't do the cemetery at night, as it was a church. One of the women did stay the night, but the other had to go home after her caregiver called.

The next morning the woman came downstairs to tell her something did happen.

"I got up to go to the bathroom and I saw this soldier standing by the door. He asked me if I needed anything, but I couldn't answer him... I was that dumbfounded. For the first time, I get a man asking if I need anything and I can't say a word! Then he vanished."

Around what Dot thought was 2001, all of the rooms had been rented out. All the people renting them had arrived but one. When a woman and her husband arrived, Dot assumed these were the people she'd been waiting for.

The woman asked her in an abrupt manner. "Do you have activity here? You do have spirits here! I am here for a rest and I can't be bothered. They gravitate to me."

The woman and her husband had rented their room for three days. After the first night, she talked to Dot. Her husband stayed nearby.

"What's the matter?" Dot asked.

"I stayed up all night talking to Civil War soldier ghosts. They wanted me to help them get to where they wanted to go. One of them is an Aaron B. Young."

Dot told her that maybe she shouldn't stay the other two nights as she was not happy, but the woman said that it had all been paid for. I found out it had been a gift certificate someone gave her. The woman was a minister and also had ESP. She could communicate with ghosts, so besides helping her flock of living, she had the not-living to contend with too.

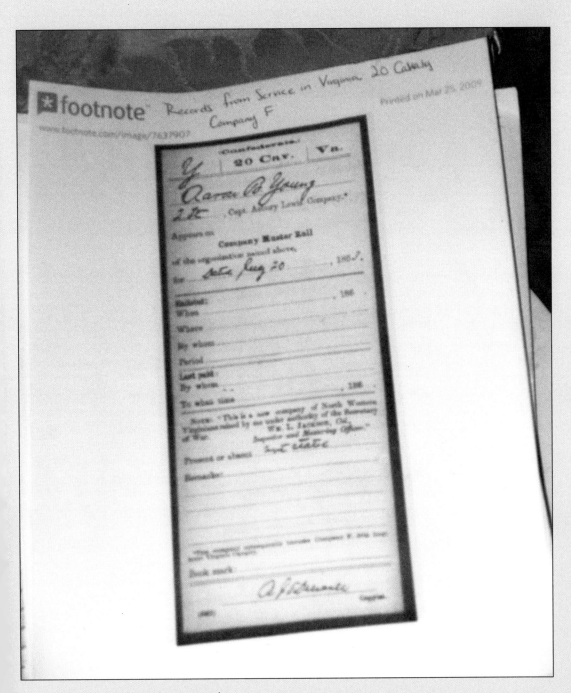

Paper with Aaron B. Young's name on it.

When the television show "Ghost Hunters" came to do an investigation at Edgewood, Dot mentioned this minister. One of the investigators went over to Berkeley Plantation to use their library and see if she could find if there had been a Confederate soldier named Aaron B. Young...and did find him listed in the records.

When the show aired in August 2009, Guy Young saw it and contacted Edgewood. It seemed that Aaron B. Young was his great-great grandfather. He wanted to see the paper that I also saw, with Aaron's name on it. Funny thing about this is that Aaron did not die in the war, but of old age in Wirt County, West Virginia, on March 15, 1913. He had served as a lieutenant in the 20th Virginia Calvary for the Confederacy in 1863 and later was promoted to captain. The middle initial "B" was for Bell.

The Author's Experience

Despite their EMF meters going off at a tricycle, not much happened to the ghost hunters that night. I know that sometimes a single night is not enough to catch anything — if anything wants to be caught. Nothing came out in the pictures I took and most of what I recorded were the voices of Dot, myself, Candy, and the man who rented Lizzie's room. There was one spot where I was alone in the dining room and I could hear the faint sound of a woman's voice. It was not Dot or Candy, as their voices were audible in the background from the kitchen. No, this sounded much closer. Is it Lizzie? I can't say, but it was the only evidence I caught that day.

I heard about other people's experiences. One woman went to Edgewood with her son. She found the place to be charming. Candy was the one who showed her around that day. They heard noises downstairs, but no one was there, and her son saw shadows in Lizzie's bedroom.

Another woman and her husband have enjoyed weekend getaways at Edgewood on five occasions in the past six years. A paranormal occurrence happened to them during a stay in February 2006. They were awakened in the middle of the night by the sound of a woman softly humming a tune at the foot of the bed. They thought it was a music box at first, but there wasn't one in the room. A peculiar sound also came to them from the window. After the humming stopped, both tried to get back to sleep — except loud noises of what sounded like heavy furniture being dragged across the floor kept them awake. Her husband did not believe in ghosts before, but after that night, he became a firm believer!

Next time you need a weekend getaway, try Edgewood Plantation Bed and Breakfast. You will be treated right and all the rooms are comfortable for your stay. Just don't be shocked if in the middle of the night you're awakened by the rustling of petticoats. That's just Lizzie.

For information on renting one of the rooms, even Lizzie's, or to make a reservation to take one of their tours, visit Edgewood's website at www.edgewoodplantation.com or call 1-804-829-2962.

Is this Lizzie Rowland in the Westover Parish Church Cemetery?

WESTOVER PLANTATION

A National Historic Landmark, Westover was built circa 1730 by William Byrd II. Born March 28, 1674, William II was the son of Mary Horsmanden Byrd and William Byrd I, a Virginia planter and son of an English goldsmith. It was William Byrd I who purchased the land that the house was built on. Besides a place to live, the house also signified his political and social aspirations. William II was married twice; first to Lucy Parke from Virginia and then after she died in England of smallpox in 1716, he married Maria Taylor. Byrd died away from home on August 26, 1744 while president of the Virginia Council of State and was buried at Westover. In addition to being a published writer, he is also considered the founder of Richmond.

Westover Plantation House.

Legend has it that this well was used to escape Indian
attacks as it led down to a tunnel to the river.

Westover was named for Henry West, fourth Lord of Delaware and son of Thomas West, Governor of Virginia. Byrd did not have it built in wood, but instead used brick. It is considered perhaps a premier example of American colonial Georgian architecture.

The shady tulip poplars framing the building are more than 150 years old. The roof is unusually steep, with tall chimneys in pairs at both ends. An elaborate doorway is recognized as "the Westover doorway" despite its adaptation to many other buildings. Westover's two wings were once upon a time identical, and part of the three-story central structure. The east wing had housed the famous Byrd library, containing 4,000 volumes. It burned during the War Between the States. The present east wing was built about 1900, and both wings were connected to the main home at that time.

There is an ice-house and a dry well in another small building on the property. The well leads to a passageway, or tunnel, that snaked underneath the house to the river. It was used to escape from the Indians. Across the driveway from the ice-house is the Necessary House.

The property remained in the Byrd family until 1817. In 1899, Mrs. Clarise Sears Ramsey, a Byrd descendent, bought the property and had it restored. Mr. and Mrs. Richard Crane purchased it in 1921. The place is still in the hands of the Fisher family. A preservation easement was placed on 636 acres in 1974.

Is It Haunted?

Besides being of historical significance, Westover is almost reputed to be haunted by three phantoms. The first one concerns Evelyn Byrd, daughter of William Byrd II. When the girl turned 10 years old, her father sent her to England to be schooled. It was in England later on that Evelyn fell in love with a man. Many historians believe him to be Charles Morduant. The legend goes on to say her father forbade the union. With a heavy heart, she returned to Westover in 1726, forgetting the romance. William Byrd would live to regret his decision because it is said that Evelyn died of a broken heart in 1737.

Evelyn is buried what could be a family cemetery, up the river a quarter-mile west of the house. So is William Byrd I and his wife, the former Mary. There is also, according to some historians, the third oldest known tombstone in America there. It belongs to Captain William Perry, who died August 6, 1637.

It was at the cemetery that Patty Ceran had felt something brush her arm while taking pictures. Thinking it was a spiderweb, she went to check, but found nothing. She believes Westover is definitely haunted.

Others have had experiences over the years too. Some claimed to get a feeling of being watched when walking the path around the house while others admitted to hearing a woman's voice. Is it Evelyn Byrd, or the other female spirit that haunts the house?

There is two more spirits that roam the house. One of them is Elizabeth Hill-Carter, who married William Byrd III. The other is William Byrd III himself.

Elizabeth had grown up at Shirley Plantation. She left it when she wedded William. After twelve years of marriage to him and five children, she found that she did not trust him to be faithful to her. She searched through clothing in a clothes press on the third floor, looking for proof of his infidelities. Instead the clothes press fell on her, killing her. She is said to haunt the third floor to this day.

Evelyn Byrd's tomb.

William married Mary Willow, who he had been cheating with on his first wife, shortly after. The Carters did not like this and gave her the nickname of Willing Mary. William did not give up his gambling ways and committed suicide in 1777 in his bedroom on the third floor. His wraith haunts the bedroom he killed himself in. To me it is strange that a man kills himself on the same floor his first wife's ghost haunts. Could she have, in a way, driven him to his death?

On Sunday, March 7, 2010, I found myself doing what countless other tourists have done before me. I took my own self-guided tour after slipping my money in a box for it at the famous Westover gates. The gates have William Byrd's initials in the ironwork and the eagles on the gateposts are a play on the name "Byrd." The wrought-iron fence has supporting columns topped by unusual stone finials cut to resemble an acorn for perseverance (from little acorns great oaks grow); a pineapple for hospitality, a Greek Key to the World for knowledge; a cornucopia, or horn of plenty: a beehive for industry; and an urn of flowers for beauty.

I ambled into the grounds where the house stood. I walked a path that led to the formal gardens. At the center of where the paths cross, I found a tomb with its interesting epitaph that honored William Byrd I, "Black Swan of Westover," buried there in 1744.

Some people drove up in a truck to help a female tenant move. She had rented from the Fishers. After we talked, I left them to their moving and walked into a small structure nearby. I turned on my digital recorder to hopefully catch some EVPs and took pictures. I also used my KII meter from time to time. I think I did get something in the ice-house. After the people had left and I was alone by the house, I felt as if someone or something was watching me from the house.

I walked away from the house, down the path, and through the gates. I followed the dirt path that led to the cemetery about a quarter of a mile away. There had been signs posted that you couldn't drive down it, so I felt glad I had worn good walking shoes that day. It was a fine day for a walk. I saw a couple having a picnic near the river; they waved. I waved back. Not as long of a walk as I feared, I found the cemetery, surrounded by an ironwork fence — except for two old tombs that laid side-by-side away from the fenced in cemetery. One was still complete while the other's top had been broken.

In the fenced cemetery, I found Evelyn Byrd's tomb. I left my recorder on top of it to see if I would get anything on audio and went over to the other two tombs to take pictures. I didn't get anything. It seems that Evelyn, and even Benjamin Harrison, one of the others with a tomb there, didn't feel the need to hang around where their remains lie.

I left the spot and headed back to my car, as Sherwood Plantation was next on my list. I left Westover to its ghosts.

Westover is located at 7000 Westover Road on the south side of Virginia Route 5, six miles west of Charles City. Just follow the dirt road that goes to Berkley, taking the left when it splits. The place is open for self-guided tours of the grounds only.

Dancing With The Devil

"Once you are dancing with the devil, the prettiest capers won't help you."
— E. T. A. Hoffmann

Just like Daniel Webster took on the Devil in folklore, another man also challenged the Devil: Colonel Philip Lightfoot. A real person who lived from 1689 to 1748, Lightfoot was the ancestor of Harry Lightfoot Lee and the Confederate general, Robert E. Lee. He also owned some land in what is known today as Charles City, which, according to the legends, the Devil himself laid claim to.

Bordering the James River and called Dancing Point, nothing grew on it for centuries, though the land all around it proved to be fertile and productive. Gardening experts today would say that something logical caused the problem, but that wouldn't be romantic — not like the legend.

Legend says that the Devil caused the barrenness and remarked that the land was his, not Lightfoot's. Colonel Lightfoot agreed to a contest between the two of them. They would see who was the best dancer and could last the longest, with the land as the prize. They marched to Dancing Point at dusk and shed their coats and tricorns. After building a large fire, both proceeded to dance their hearts out. Well, no doubt, Lightfoot did. The Devil wouldn't have a heart, now would he?

Around and around a tree stump they whirled. Lightfoot had claims to being an accomplished dancer and he proved it that night. The Devil didn't give up, as he was determined to win, but when the first rays of dawn painted the morning sky, the Devil knew he had lost. He limped away in humiliation, crossing the James River to Surry County. The old-timers report that he still lives there.

The legend doesn't end there, as there are those who say they see flickering lights. When they venture closer, the witnesses profess that they have seen two spectral figures dancing away furiously.

Guess Philip Lightfoot hasn't rested easy in his grave, but continues to dance to beat the Devil.

Jeb Stuart Rides Again

I figured this had to be in Charles City County somewhere; after all, he did stop at Edgewood on his way to Richmond. So this story is in the Charles City section.

Known as "Jeb," Stuart was probably the most famous cavalryman of the Civil War. Struck down at age 31 by a Union sharpshooter's bullet, his exploits during the Civil War made the stuff of legends, except they were real. His full name was James Ewell Brown Stuart.

There was the time he rode one night into Stonewall Jackson's camp, unbuckled his saber, and climbed into Jackson's bed. Jackson retorted, "General Stuart, I am always glad to see you here. You might select better hours sometimes . . . but General, you must not get into my bed with your boots and spurs on and ride me around like a cavalry horse at night!"

Stuart became mortally wounded at the Battle of Yellow Tavern near Ashland on May 11, 1864. Taken to the home of his brother-in-law, Charles Brewer, on West Grace Street in Richmond, he passed away May 12, 1864, at 7:30 p.m. The next day he was buried in Hollywood Cemetery, attended by President Jefferson Davis and hundreds of local residents.

The ghostly ride of Stuart's historic crossing of the Chickahominy that supposedly he takes is a reenactment of one he did in 1862. In 1962, two Virginia couples picnicked at the very spot. One of the men was Bill Latane — the great, great grandson of Captain William Latane, who had rode with Stuart during that fateful ride. What phenomenon Latane and the others witnessed that day has been recorded and was published in Nancy Roberts's Civil War ghost book.

The other man with Latane, Edmund Farley, wandered away to search for clues to where the Forge Bridge may have been. He became sleepy and lay down to fall asleep. When he woke up, he heard noise like men building a bridge, but no one was there! He then noticed a figure dressed in a Confederate officer uniform with a yellow sash and black thigh high boots lying on the ground. Thinking the man was dead, Farley touched him and found him breathing. The man had a black felt hat with a long plume tucked under its band and a beautiful sword. The man's eyes opened and he smiled. He told Farley that his men were working hard on building the bridge in time before the Yankees came — and if they were not finished in time, then they would have excitement. Farley ambled away, wondering if he hadn't stepped into a historical time warp, but more than likely a reenactment was going on.

The others had their own experience. They saw a troop of Confederates on horseback, led by the same figure Farley had seen on the ground. He noticed Union soldiers too. Latane wondered if a reenactment was going on. Just then he saw something white on the ground and bent over to pick it up and saw that it was a white handkerchief. Strangely enough, it had his initials, "W. L." Just then he watched as they charged and one of them struck a federal officer in the neck and was shot, falling to the ground. As it looked too realistic to be a reenactment, Latane wondered if he had witnessed his ancestor's demise. Just then he noticed blood on the handkerchief he held. He looked up to see a convoy of modern military vehicles. The soldiers had vanished.

Later Latane took his handkerchief to a museum and had it authenticated as a genuine Civil War artifact. As for Farley, he contacted authorities about a reenactment that day, but was told it had been cancelled due to the military convoy that was to travel through there that day.

Chapter Six

GLOUCESTER

Gloucester lies south of Williamsburg. When Bill drove us over the bridge where we stopped to pay our toll to enter the town, we found a nice, quiet place.

Formed in 1651 in the Virginia Colony, it was named for Henry Stuart, Duke of Gloucester, the third son of King Charles I of Great Britain. Located in the Middle Peninsula region, it borders the York River and the lower Chesapeake Bay. It was the site of Werawocomoco, a capital of the Native American group known as the Powhatan Confederacy.

In the 1600s and 1700s, Gloucester was a tobacco producing area. There are many old plantation homes and magnificent private estates that remain today in perfect condition. Others are nothing more than ruins like the Rosewell Plantation.

Gloucester is where Thomas Jefferson spent many nights with his friend John Page at Rosewell. Both George Washington and Thomas Jefferson worshipped at Abingdon Episcopal Church. Other notable residents of the area include John Buckner, who, in 1680, brought the colony its first printing press; botanist Dr. Walter Reed conquered yellow fever during the building of the Panama Canal; T. C. Walker, though born in slavery, broke those chains and became one of Gloucester's first and most respected successful African-American businessman; and Robert R. Moton successfully fought and lobbied for an African American to be appointed as an assistant to the Secretary of War.

Besides the Beaver Dam Park, the county has the Museum of History housed in the Botetourt Building, formerly the Botetourt Hotel. This place was built in the late eighteenth century as a roadside tavern or ordinary and was known as John New's Ordinary.

In addition to being a nice rural town with a long and notable history, Gloucester has something else. It has ghosts.

ROSEWELL PLANTATION

Located on the banks of the York River, in Gloucester County, Rosewell was built in 1725. It was home for one hundred years to the Page family. Rosewell was considered the finest example of Georgian architecture in the country. When Mann Page died in the front hall before the completion of the place, there was a legend that claimed "God struck him down for his excess." Rosewell was excessive, even by grand planter standards. It is said that eight men are able to walk abreast with bayonets up the staircase. The halls were paneled in mahogany and the floors were of Italian marble.

One of the Pages, John Page, son of the builder, attended the College of William and Mary with Thomas Jefferson. One can imagine what the two thought of for an emerging nation in which both played crucial parts.

When you visit the place, you'll see mostly ruins. Four chimneys rise like fingers pointing to the sky. There's also the east wall with a window and the wine cellar. Enough of the walls remain to get a sense of how big the place had been in all its glory. The graveyard for the family is off to the side of the house as part of the extensive grounds.

It is said that the family still held balls and parties in the Great Hall, even during the lean times following the War Between the States. It took a fire in 1916 to bring down this once magnificent mansion, leaving it a shell of itself. Still, that a shell remained to this day is proof of the craftsmanship of the eighteenth century. The last family to own it donated the site in 1979 to the Gloucester Historical Society. It was in 1995 that the Rosewell Foundation took over to preserve and study this piece of history. Today, one can visit this place. It has an exhibit hall, gift shop, and archeology lab. For hours and directions, visit their website at www.rosewell.org.

The tombs of the original Page family had been moved to Abingdon Episcopal Church. The bodies themselves are still buried at Rosewell. No explanation for why only the tombs were removed and not the bodies, except some of the other family members are laid to rest in the church cemetery.

Ruins of the Rosewell Plantation house.

There is a sweet family legend attached to the plantation. It is said that John and Margaret Lowther Page's courtship began with the exchange of poems.

John was a widower in 1790 and served in the First Congress of the United States that met in New York that year. He met Margaret there. She was thirty at the time. According to the tale, he had escorted her to a party and discovered later that she had left her glove back in his carriage. He ran out to get it and had it sent back to her with a note.

The note mentioned that taking "G" from glove meant love and that he offered that to her. Of course, she sent him a reply, saying that "Taking "P" from 'Page' leaves 'Age.'" She ended that he was too old for her. Whether she was only teasing him, or had a change of heart, the couple did marry some months later — and they kept exchanging notes the rest of their married life.

The Ghosts

Many of the supernatural accounts of Rosewell were not as romantic. Music (like from a harpsichord) is heard playing, guests are seen descending down invisible stairs, boys with lanterns stand where doorways once were, and a woman in a red cloak rushes into a rose garden. Also reported are drops in temperature by a good fifteen degrees or more and strange noises. Some of the phenomena are sounds that seem like slaves coming in from the fields. One young woman reported hearing strange noises on the back trails and came back to the plantation quickly. Later she tried to say that maybe it had been animals.

The front steps witnesses had seen the ghost lady come down.

There are stories that tell of a young woman observed walking down the front steps every night, only to vanish. One of the eeriest tales is of a couple who found their exit blocked by a car with 1930s plates. They also saw a pale woman peering through the back window.

For Patty Ceran and her family, nothing out of the ordinary happened when they visited Rosewell, except for some noises coming from the basement when they peered into it. They never could explain the sounds.

Another encounter happened to a young woman and some of her friends at the ruins late one night. They didn't trespass on the property, but stayed on the gravel road that led up to the gates. They left the place in a panic when they heard voices and what they thought sounded like horses trotting down the drive.

Someone else had taken her kids to the place to learn about history. Her eldest child walked back into the woods to go find where the old ice cellar had been. The girl hung around the back of the cellar when she heard the sound of horses and gravel "churning." Her mother, her siblings, and she were the only people there that day...at least, the only "living" visitors!

Back in the late 1970s, three teenagers drove in a truck to Rosewell one night to check the place out because of the ghost stories. They parked in front of the mansion, maybe about a hundred feet or so from the front steps. The night was pitch black, with no moon. As their eyes adjusted to the darkness, they noticed two red lights in front of them. They thought that maybe they were the taillights of a car parked in front of them, but that was impossible since they were alone there. Finally two of the three decided that it had to be a car and that obviously they weren't alone. Someone else had parked there too, and they just missed it driving up.

Then the lights began to levitate. Astonished, they asked each other if what they were seeing actually was happening. They asked the third person, but he never answered them. They began to wonder if someone was fooling with them. After all, how could a light climb as high as a tree limb? They thought maybe it could be a boat on the York River since the river was in that general direction behind the Rosewell Mansion, but the river was too far away from the mansion. Besides, the vegetation and forest would obscure the view. More lights appeared and they darted around the tree limbs in front of the mansion stairs. They enjoyed it, when all of sudden their friend, who hadn't said a word, started the pickup truck and threw it into reverse. He drove through a cornfield, with the other two bouncing around in the bed of the truck.

To this day, the third friend claims he saw nothing, but the others know better. He saw something more than the lights they saw that night. What it was, he won't say.

Another witness told of hearing someone going up and down the steps. Yet, she saw no one! Another person who lives in Gloucester mentioned visiting Rosewell one time at night. He and his friends like to go out there to do a bit of paranormal investigating. There were four of them at the time; two guys and two girls, all with their own flashlights. The guys went in the cellar first and then the girls walked in after them. All the flashlights dimmed, and one of the other guys freaked out, saying he saw a guy standing on each side of them. The witness admitted that it felt as if they were being escorted. He has never gone back. He also mentioned that if you go over by the ice hole and look at the mansion, it looks like a man is sitting on one of the ledges.

There have been other paranormal investigators at Rosewell, mainly at night. I watched one group's video, but to me, except for one orb, the rest looked like raindrops.

Those who work at the place do offer some explanations that debunk some of the ghost stories, such as the evidence that rats were found living in the walls when the ruins were excavated. As for the couple that claimed an old car blocked the drive, a worker said someone *living* in the area had parked it there.

The Author's Experience

Bill and I went to Rosewell on Saturday, April 17. I thought it was going to rain, but by the time we reached Gloucester it became cloudy, with some sun. Not too bad of a spring day, except for the pollen that had hit Virginia since end of March with a vengeance.

Close to 10 a.m. we turned into the unpaved road that led to Rosewell. We caught sight of the Visitor's Center after noticing that the closed gate across the road that kept people from going to the ruins.

Once the worker came to open the gate, we drove down to the ruins and parked the Toyota in a field between a field of what looked like dry, dead corn stalks and the ruins itself. I thought that this debunked the explanation of a neighbor's car being the spook vehicle as the place was surrounded by fields (which I suspected the Rosewell Foundation might rent out to someone to plant) and woods. The nearest neighbor is not close at all, so unless it was a tourist's car... Who knows?

I grabbed my bookbag with my equipment in it and slung my camera around my neck and stepped out of the car. The chimneys of the ruins seem to reach for the sky and looked imposing, even in its skeleton state. Though I did get a few pictures of it, nothing seemed spookier than the framed one I saw hanging in the Visitor's Center, where someone had gotten a photograph of it in the fog. I sloshed through wet grass over to the sign where the family cemetery had been once upon a time. From there I headed over to the room, stopping by what was left of one of its outbuildings to snap a picture. Finally I stood in front of the ruins, taking a few pictures. I drew closer and picked my way over bricks, finding the entrance to the basement. I had been advised by Patty Ceran to do some recording in there and maybe capture some EVPs. I entered into a cool, dark cave-like place. More worried about spiders than ghosts, as I listened to a bee buzzing in there, I snapped a few pictures with my camera and then took my recorder out of my bookbag.

I clicked it on and asked some questions, hoping to get something to answer me. I did it for ten minutes. For most of the time, except for the buzzing insect, I heard nothing. Then for a second, I thought I heard a woman's voice, very faint. I couldn't make out what she said. I knew that Bill and I were the only ones in the area. I shut off the recorder and left the basement. I wanted to see if anyone else came since we had, but I found no one else — just me and Bill. I hoped that maybe I gotten that faint voice on my recorder.

I walked around what had been the inside of the house, snapping more pictures. I saw that a Kenny J and Sherry T had scratched their names and the date, October 1, 1977, on the wall of what I think is one of the chimneys. I even climbed up what I think were the steps that led up to the back of the house and used my recorder for five minutes. Then, picking my way off of what could have been the foyer or maybe the back porch, I walked back into the woods, crunching dirt on the path that led to the brick ice-house. I found a fenced in area and took a few more pictures of what was left of it.

The basement entrance.

Fenced-in brick ice house
in woods behind the ruins.

Orb in basement—
against wall at right.

I saw that it was almost 11 a.m. and knew we had to be at a party in Yorktown at noon, so I hurried on the path back to our car. I heard sounds, but dismissed them as birds and animals hidden in the trees and bushes. I don't think anything ghostly watched me.

I snapped a few more pictures, climbed back into the passenger side of the car, and we drove away. We passed a woman and her young son walking down the dirt road, a familiar Rosewell Plantation map in the boy's hands, and waved back as the woman waved at us. I wondered if they might even see one of the former residents still hanging around the ruins. Still, it was good to see someone taking their child to learn about Virginia's past, ghosts or no ghosts.

At the party, I uploaded my photos to my laptop and then enjoyed the party food and my friends. The next day, in the morning, I listened to my EVPs. At one point, where I had asked for some kind of sound, even footsteps, I caught the faint tap-tap of what sounded like footsteps walking away! It wasn't me as I had been very still, hoping to get something, anything. Later, I found that I did capture the mysterious woman's faint voice. Whoever she was, she even said something again a few seconds later. I couldn't make out any of the words, just that it was feminine. I didn't get anything on the second session. I did catch an orb in the basement, but nothing else odd in any of the other photos I took.

Rosewell may be nothing but ruins, but something still haunts it. Next time you tour it and hear a voice when no one is around or see something white flitting out of the corner of your eye, it's just the former residents welcoming into their home.

From Tears to Flowers

There is a tragic tale connected to a ghost story set in a house called Church Hill in Gloucester County. In 1650, Mordecai Cooke received a grant of 1,174 acres of land. He built a brick house on the site in 1658, and it became known as Mordecai's Mount. The place caught fire in the 1700s and only a brick wing remained. Much later this part also burned, and a new frame house was built over the site, becoming Church Hill. The property was inherited by the Throckmortons, descendents of Cooke.

One descendent was Elizabeth Throckmorton. The strangest part of this story is there is no record of this young woman. In the tale, her father took her to London, where she met an English gentleman and fell in love with him. The love-struck couple declared eternal faithfulness to one another. Both promised to correspond by mail their wedding plans, but her father was dead set against the match and intercepted the mail, determined she would never hear from her young man. Elizabeth became ill and died. The legend claims that she pined for her beloved and lost the will to live. Whatever was the true reason, on one windy day in November, the family buried her in the family graveyard.

That same night, the family butler, angry from some slight done to him by the family, dug up her coffin in hopes of stealing any jewels that had been buried with her. When he tried to yank a ring off a finger and couldn't, he sawed the finger off!

The dead girl hadn't really died, but lay in a catatonic state. The pain from her cut finger revived her. Terrified by what he thought was a dead girl raising from her grave, the servant bolted, never to be heard from again.

Barefoot and dressed only in a thin gown, Elizabeth climbed out of the grave — just as a terrible snowstorm arose. She tottered out of the graveyard and made for the house. When she got to the front door, she scratched at it, but no one heard her. They discovered her frozen body the next morning, covered by the snow, at the end of a trail of bloody footprints coming from the garden. Though the snow blanketed the ground, the footsteps had not been erased.

It is said that after the first snowfall of the year, sounds of rustling skirts ascending the staircase can be heard, followed by logs being placed in the fireplaces in the house, and then fire crackling. On investigations, not one log or fire is found in any of the fireplaces. More alarming, traces of blood are evident in the pristine snow, a red trail leading from the graveyard to the house.

Another facet of this ghost story is when Julius Browne, Jr. rode past the place on horseback one night. To his amazement, he saw the place ablaze with lights, even though he knew that the owner, Professor Warner Taliaferro, was gone. He assumed that maybe his sisters might have taken shelter there, since they hadn't gotten home yet, and he set his horse for the place. Servants from their living quarters on the property believed that Professor Taliaferro had returned home. Neither he nor Browne's sisters were found in the house or on the property anywhere.

One more aspect of the ghostly visitations is about the violets that grow more beautiful and lush near the steps to Church Hill than anywhere else on the property. The story goes on to say that maybe the dying girl's tears had fallen on the snow in those spots... tears that gave life to beauty in sadness.

OTHER HAUNTINGS
OF GLOUCESTER COUNTY

"The tender word forgotten, The letter you did not write, The flower you might have sent, dear, Are your haunting ghosts tonight." — Margaret Elizabeth Sangster

White Marsh Plantation

There are over a 1,500 slaves buried in a graveyard in the peach orchard on White Marsh Plantation. It is they who it is believe contribute to many of the phenomena on this land since after the Civil War. And when they did renovations on the house in 1948, the apparition of the original woman of the house, Evalina Tabb, was seen. She would be caught folding children's clothing near a chest of drawers in one of the bedrooms. Another time, someone felt something brushed against them on the stairs and the swishing sound of Evalina's taffeta skirts can be heard in the hallway. Built by the Tabb family in 1750s, today it is a private residence along the Ware River.

A Ghostly Encounter

Recorded in *Stories of Old Gloucester* by Caroline Baytop Sinclair, there is a story set during the Civil War, concerning Abingdon Church. On a dark, stormy night in 1862, a lone Federal cavalryman returned from his station at Gloucester Point. Separated from his troop, he stumbled upon the church. Cold, tired, wet, and miserable, he and his horse sought shelter. He led his horse inside. Obviously just vacated by troops, the place was in disorder. He saw pews and paneling broken and charred wood and ashes scattered along the stone floor.

As he stood there, he sensed something. He spied movement in the north gallery thanks to the intermittent light from the lightning. Something white and tall descended the stairway. Just then another bolt of lightning flashed and he saw a filmy human-like apparition. He could see through it!

Frightened, the soldier mounted his steed and crashed through the door and across the churchyard, but when another flash of lightning streaked across the sky and lit up the area, he looked back and saw that someone had hitched a ride with him on his horse.

An interesting note to this was that I found online that one paranormal group had investigated the church. They wanted to see if it was really haunted, and got an EVP and one photo with an orb.

She Saw a Soldier!

One of the volunteers at the Rosewell Visitor Center told me a story of a little girl of the owner of a store off Route 17 in Gloucester. It seems that one night she saw the phantoms of some soldiers there and, frightened, ran out of the place and down the steps, yelling she saw them. This was quite some time ago and the woman is not even sure that the store is still there.

Murder or Accident at Paynton Hall

Legend has it that spirits still roamed the grounds of where Paynton Hall once stood. Built by Fairfax Dalton in the early 1700s, he lived there with his wife, Lettitia and their daughter, Caro. The story goes that both he and Caro fought and that it was Lettitia that may be behind their "accidental deaths." Is it true? Had she done it to get some peace in her life? Whatever the truth, in 1745, a black maid later poisoned Lettitia.

Many years later bloodstains would appear on the marble landing where Fairfax fell to his death. Also a small, ghostly figure would be sighted in the 1800s. People claimed that it tried to trip them and cause accidents. Was this Lettitia?

Though the house burned to the ground, there are those who say that horrific screams emulate from the ruins to this day. You can find out for yourself as the overgrown foundation is located not far from the Rosewell Plantation and the York Plains Ford Battleground.

Chapter Seven

POQUOSON

The term "poquoson" described a boundary line between two elevated tracts of land; such a boundary contained a stream, river, or a creek with an adjoining marsh that lay between two tracts of higher ground.

Used as a common noun, Poquoson is found in many deeds along the eastern seaboard. Through the years, though, it became a proper noun for land lying between two such poquosons — the Old Poquoson River and the New Poquoson River. It was first mentioned in the Captain Christopher Calthrope land grant issued by a court in Elizabeth City on April 26, 1631. According to historians, Poquoson is the oldest, English-speaking settlement in the United States that still bears its original name. Many of those settlers were plantation owners. With their tenants and apprentices, they lived south of Back River.

There are some interesting things about this city, such as Poquoson Avenue was called "the path to the church." The church mentioned in this was the Old Charles Parish Church located in Tabb. The first movie theater in Poquoson was known as the "Thimble." Forrest Road used to be Barrel Factory Road and Hudgins Road was called Billy Goat Road. As for Wythe Creek Road, it was called "The New Road." Besides all of this history, Poquoson also has a ghostly legend attached to it.

LEGEND OF DOLLY MAMMY

"From the body of one guilty deed a thousand ghostly fears and haunting thoughts proceed." — William Wordsworth

Dusk approached and it grew windy. Torrential rain fell. Dolly Mammy was worried as the cows were still out on the marsh and they could fall in and drown. She asked her two daughters to go and bring them in, but they refused to go out in the cold and the rain.

Dolly was terrified of losing the cows and wrapped herself up as well as she could. Then she stomped off. She never returned. Since it was still night and the pouring rain made it difficult to see anything, her daughters waited until morning before they went to tell the neighbors. Surely, they figured, their mother had found some shelter and that was why she hadn't come home with the cows. A search party was formed to search the area for the missing woman. They found her, but too late. A leg stuck out of the mud at a place known as Bell's Oyster Gut. The grass that surrounded the spot had been torn away where obviously Dolly Mammy had pulled and tugged at it in a desperate attempt to get free of the mire, but it had been in vain.

Not long after Dolly's death, her daughters began to be haunted by a mysterious banging on the side of the house. It sounded as if someone was trying to knock the house down. Another story told of how the two girls' hair was braided together while they slept in their trundle bed. Others claimed that the girls' faces were scratched and that the girls' trundle bed floated in mid-air. The neighbors became terrified. The knocking and banging could be heard all throughout the area.

The army was called in to investigate these strange goings-on. The officer in charge searched the area, but found no cause for the banging and knocking. When dusk approached, he and his men joined hands and encircled the house. That is when the soldiers heard the noises. It sounded loud and very unnatural — and it scared them off.

The officer relayed the event to his wife, who suggested a medium. A séance was arranged, and the medium went into a trance. She asked that the spirit make itself known. A loud knock responded. When the spirit was asked to appear, a shadow of a woman in a rocking chair materialized on the wall. The shadow began to rock and knit. A loud, shrill moan filled the air — and then the ghost dissipated. There are other versions of this account that asserted that the séance worked. Others maintain that Dolly kept appearing. No matter which legend is told, it always ends the same. The grass no longer grows on Bell's Oyster Gut where Dolly's leg was found sticking out of the mire.

The docent at Lee Hall Mansion told me that she heard the rangers talk about this story, though she never said the ghost was Dolly Mammy. Just that sometimes they hear a woman calling for her cows, and that it is near Yorktown.

Next time you decide to walk near the marsh, beware. You just might run into Dolly Mammy.

Chapter Eight

NEWPORT NEWS

Located at the southwestern part of the Virginia Peninsula, Newport News is an independent city in Hampton Roads. It was part of Warwick County, one of the eight original shires of Virginia formed by the House of Burgesses in the British Colony of Virginia by order of King Charles I in 1634. It was mostly composed of farms and undeveloped land, at least until almost 250 years later. The original area near the mouth of the James River was first referred to as "Newportes Newes" as early as 1621. There is no known record of where the name came about.

One story is an early group of Jamestown colonists left to return to England after the Starving Time during the winter of 1609–1610. They did this aboard a ship of Captain Christopher Newport. There was an encounter with another fleet of supply ships under the new Governor Thomas West, 3rd, Baron De La Warr in the James River off Mulberry Island. The new governor ordered them to return to Jamestown. Supposedly then, the community was named for Newport's "good news." Another tale says that it may have gotten its name from an old English word "news" meaning "new town." One source claims that the "New" arose from the original settlement's being rebuilt after a fire.

There's another supposed reason too, that the original name was "New Port Newce," named for a person with the name Newce and the town's place as a new seaport. Sir William Newce was an English soldier who had settled in Ireland and sailed to Virginia with Sir Francis Wyatt in October 1621. Granted 2,500 acres of land, he died two days later. His brother, Capt. Thomas Newce, was given six hundred acres at Kequatan, now called "Elizabeth Cittie." His partner, Daniel Gookin, was the one who founded the settlement.

In 1881, Collis P. Huntington, who owned the Peninsula Extension of the Chesapeake and Ohio Railway from Richmond, provided a new pathway for the railroad to bring West Virginia bituminous coal to port for coastal shipping and worldwide export. A few years later, Huntington and his associates also built a shipyard.

In 1896, the new unincorporated town of Newport News briefly replaced Denbigh as the seat of Warwick County. It became an independent city, separating from the county, but in 1958, Newport News consolidated with the former Warwick County. Newport News was chosen as the city name.

The city has the Mariner's Museum, Virginia War Museum, Peninsula Fine Arts Center, Virginia Living Museum, and the U.S. Army Transportation Museum on the Fort Eustis grounds. It also has Endview Plantation and Lee Hall Mansion. Boxwood Inn Bed and Breakfast is within its borders. Most of all, though, it has ghosts.

BOXWOOD INN

Kathryn and her husband, Derek Hulick, along with their daughter and son-in-law, took over Boxwood Inn on December 1, 2000. She was told the place was haunted, but, as she said about the former owner, Barbara Lucas was a good salesperson. However, after she had various paranormal groups call her asking to be allowed to do an investigation and after a couple of people she had staying over told her of their experiences, she began to wonder.

Boxwood Inn is within easy reach of Williamsburg, Newport News, and Yorktown in Historic Lee Hall Village. It is a lovely bed and breakfast with the front facing train tracks. The train did stop there, in fact. In its past, it was once upon a time the home of Simon Curtis, son of Dr. Curtis of Endview Plantation.

Built around 1896, it has been the Warrick County Hall of Records, a general store, and a post office. The front door led into the general store, to the post office, and even to Simon's office. Simon's wife, Edith's, family was from up North and into antiques. When the place was empty for ten years and an auction held of what was inside, they found four million dollars' worth of antiques! Edith spent her last days there with a nurse who smoked a lot and had a raspy voice. It is said the nurse is another ghost haunting the place. In fact, a couple who one time smelled smoke in the Inn had asked if smoking was allowed there. Could this be the nurse?

Boxwood Inn Bed and Breakfast.

The building was leased by Fort Eustis for the officers during both World Wars.

After his last living relative passed away, Simon's estate was left unoccupied and the house fell to ruin. It was condemned by the city of Newport News. Then Barbara Lucas and her husband bought the place to run as a bed and breakfast. Years later, Kathryn and her husband purchased the place.

The gentle spirit here is believed to be Nannie Curtis. It is said that doors open and close all by themselves. Nannie is also blamed for knocking on doors in the morning. Apparently she does not believe in sleeping late. There are also stories that a phantom of an elderly gentleman with a cane has been spotted.

When I stopped there on March 11, 2010 on my way down to Virginia Beach, Kathy told me that there are a total of seven ghosts counted as haunting the place. There have been two investigations done by RTL Paranormal. The first time, they shared the investigation with a group from Glen Allen, Virginia. The second time they came alone and let Kathy and Derek join in.

Kathy said that guests have told her that ghosts are always following her — and the night of the investigation was no exception. On one of the recordings, her name was called out.

Another time an EVP captured something in the parlor, which was Simon's office. One of them was a chair being dragged across the room, which hit one of the investigators, Tim, in his leg. When the investigators asked a question to get a rise out of the ghost or ghosts in the room, a gentle voice came back with, "Kathy?" The investigators used an EMF II meter by Kathy and got reactions — and when they took pictures of her, they got lots of orbs surrounding her.

In what is known as General Pershing's Suite, they had a lot of cold spots and weird stuff happening. Kathy has been told this is the most haunted room in the house, but she doesn't agree.

Before the first investigation, she made the group dinner. While they talked at the table, she felt a coldness starting at the front and wrapping itself around her to her back. Someone told her that it was her son, Chad, giving her a hug. Chad was her younger son, who died of a heart attack for no reason detected by doctors at age twenty-two. Boxwood Inn was his dream.

The dining room got loads of readings. When I interviewed Kathy at first in there, my EMF II meter went off a couple of times. I laid it on the table by her to see what would happen — and it didn't disappoint me. A couple of times all the lights would come on.

When they did the room called the Traveling Salesman's room, they got some EVPs. The name of the room came from a salesman who had stayed in there once. He had died there. From the recording:

Q: "What is your name?"
A: "Robert."
Q: "Did you die here?"
A: "Yes."

The Attic

In the attic, RTL did a video that not only captured some blue-black beads that came from out of nowhere, but also what looked like a child peeking at them from a corner. They also heard footsteps up there, the kind heel to toe boots make.

Becky watched the video camera while they were in the attic. At one point she heard a knocking next to her. That is when they came downstairs. She told them about the sound.

A young man who had been to the inn before came on Valentine's Day with his girlfriend and others and asked if they could go up to the attic. One of the girls began to take pictures and the young man felt something. He said, "Oh my gosh, everyone is up here, but they're angry that we're here."

A picture the girl just then took came up blank when they checked it later.

When Kathy took over the inn, she kept in her employ two people who had worked for Barbara. They told her about what happened to another former worker. The young woman had a young child she brought to the inn with her. She placed the child in a playpen in the office so she could work. All of a sudden the baby began to cry and she went to see what the matter is. A beautiful woman in a bonnet was patting the child. The employee grabbed the child and bolted out the door. She never returned.

Kathy later had a policeman from Charleston, South Carolina stay at the B&B.

He said, "Give me a sign that you're not going to haunt me."

Just then, the alarm clock went off for no reason. It did not work for two days after. Now, it works as if nothing was wrong with it — and, no, it never had to be fixed!

A month after she took over the place, Kathy was speaking to a bride and groom who were getting ready to leave. She felt something touch her hair and turned to see who did it. Later they asked why she did what she did. When she told them, they said they did not touch her at all.

There was also the time as she held a glass of wine that she felt a little tap. Was it Nannie, who was rumored to be a teetotaler? She is never disappointed that things happen in the dining room. Always when places are set on tables, there's sure to be a fork missing or placed somewhere else.

One morning in their own quarters, she awoke to footsteps coming from above the room, from the attic.

She thought, 'Why is Derek in the attic?'

Kathy got out of bed and walked into the living room, where she found Derek on the couch.

"What were you doing?"

"What?"

"Were you in the attic?"

"No."

The Author Takes a Tour

After we finished talking in the dining room, Kathy took me on a tour of the inn. I left the recorder on. We passed the hallway, where I stopped to take a couple of pictures, and then I followed her into Simon's office. It was cold in there, and grew even colder during the time we spent in there. I used my EMF meter to see if I could get Simon, or someone else to make the lights come on, but no such luck. I took a few pictures and kept recording.

Orbs in the hallway: one is in the chair, the other is by the floor.

Fake flower that appeared out of nowhere, along with a red one, too.

Kathryn Hulick by a trunk full of historical things in attic.

Kathy told me that Simon had been not only Treasurer, but magistrate and ran the post office and general store, too. During the Depression, Simon would buy people's notes at the bank and work with them so they would not lose their homes. He was a good man, well liked. Later on, as I listened to the recording, I heard some odd swish-swish sound for a couple seconds. Was that something supernatural? I couldn't be sure. I know that neither Kathy nor I made the noise, and the only other two people in the inn were up at the top of the staircase working on a door.

Next, she took me to the General Store. People like to hang around the place. From there we went to the area where the weddings take place at Boxwood. Supposedly, lots of activity happens there, but Kathy has never experienced anything.

We climbed the stairs to the second floor. She introduced me to the two men. One of them owned a very haunted house in Hampton. An elderly man has been seen there. For most of the time, he lives in New York, but when he is in the Hampton house and things act up, he tells them, "Work with me, or I'll sell you!" Things calm down then.

We entered the Politician's Suite first. It was in here that a guest had just used the water in the sink in the bathroom and shut it off, turning to leave. When he turned back to look, though, the cold water faucet came on, water splashing out of it. When Kathy sat in a chair and the sensitive working with RTL sat on the bed, an EVP caught a voice, but they couldn't make out what it said.

We walked over to Miss Nannie's room next. Behind the door, Kathy has an original dress that they found the bottom half all twisted up and hard to untangle. She tried to replicate how it was done, but couldn't.

We stepped into the Traveling Salesman's room. I asked some questions, hoping that he would answer me.

"Robert, did you die here? If you're not Robert, can you tell me your name?"

I got nothing on the recording from that room.

General Pershing's Suite was our last destination before heading up to the attic. Kathy had me go in first. Instead of the cold spots others felt, it was warmer actually. Though for a while I did feel cold and told Kathy. I ask whoever haunted that room to make the lights on my EMF meter blink. Of course, not one light came on.

Kathy told me that another author, Gina Farris, rented the room on purpose. She admitted to feeling a lot of cold spots that night in there. She was writing an eBook on haunted hotels and bed and breakfasts and Boxwood Inn was one of them.

Kathy owns two cats, Chelsea and Kramer. The one cat stayed away, but Kramer shadowed us, even up the stairs to the attic. Kathy tried to get him not to follow us in, but the cat did anyway. Her mind got off Kramer when she found the straw hat she uses to play a game with the ghosts was moved again from its spot. She put it back. She also noticed that all the beads from the investigation had vanished. As she took me through the different rooms in the attic and showed me what was in some of the trunks and chests up there, she kept searching for any of the beads. She did not find even one. I got to see the old school books and homework, clothing and other things in the attic. I took photographs and teased the spirits to use my EMF meter and make the lights come on for us. They had nothing to do with the meter.

Finally, ready to leave, I helped Kathy search for the missing Kramer. I halted at an indentation on the attic floor, not far from where the chest of school books and the straw hat was. I saw a blossom from what I found was an artificial flower. It had not been there when we first came into the attic. Nearby, was a red one from a fake flower. I took a picture of the white one and then picked it up and handed it to Kathy. The ghosts wanted to let me know they were there.

This big orb (at the top) was in the attic.

An orb rests on the screen in the attic.

I thanked Kathy for letting me talk to her and headed to the parking lot where my car was to head down to Virginia Beach, where I would be all weekend for a paranormal conference in the Cavalier on the Hill Hotel. I didn't get to listen to anything or check pictures until I got back home. I am not sure, but as I brought the window closer and closer, I think I saw a face there. I don't think it was Kathy. Was it Miss Nannie, checking out the stranger taking pictures of the Inn?

Need a great place to stay? Somewhere where the atmosphere is super and you'll get a good night's sleep? Check out the Boxwood, but take warning... You might be sharing your room with someone *unseen*.

Orbs in a part of the attic.

LEE HALL PLANTATION

Bill turned right and drove the Corolla up the dirt road to the parking lot behind the house of Lee Hall Plantation. It was November 21, 2009. He slid into a parking spot and shut off the engine. We stared at the mansion. It looked pretty impressive on the outside. Even if it failed to produce any paranormal activity, it was still worth a look for its obvious history.

Lee Hall is one of the last remaining antebellum homes on the Virginia Peninsula — Italian Greek Revival with a Georgian style floor. In fact, it is the only large antebellum plantation house remaining on the lower Virginia Peninsula. Only some things that are original remain, like the three plaster sunflower medallions in the ceiling, the hardwood pine floor, banisters, and doors.

Built between 1851 and 1859, the place was home to affluent planter Richard Decauter Lee (of the York County Lee family), his wife Martha, and their children, along with her two half-sisters. Three years after the house's completion, the Lees fled their home, as the Peninsula became one of the first battlegrounds of the Civil War.

Between April and May of 1862, the house was used as a Confederate headquarters by Major General John B. Magruder and General Joseph E. Johnston. A small skirmish was fought on the property by retreating Confederates and the Union cavalry on May 4, 1862. You can even see an earthwork on the property. The Lees came back and resided in the house until 1871. Since then, many different individuals have owned Lee Hall Mansion.

The City of Newport News purchased the mansion and fifteen acres in 1996, restoring the house to its antebellum appearance. The outdoor kitchen still stands behind the house, to the side. Though the Lees had slaves, none of the slave cabins were obviously on the fifteen acres the city bought — if they even survived to the twentieth century at all.

Richard had a total of seven children with Martha, but three did not survive infancy. When Martha married Richard, she brought her two sons, John and William, from her first marriage to John Young, who had drowned in the James River. As I stated earlier, she also brought two younger half-sisters with her.

Richard is not related to General Robert E. Lee. They performed a DNA test about three or four years ago to prove it.

Where we entered the house had been the English-styled basement and was now used for the office, museum, and gift shop. We paid for our tour and checked the museum out as we waited for our tour guide. When she came, we went upstairs to the first floor. She took us into the parlor, music room, and dining room. Upstairs, which was much plainer as this was the Lees' private quarters, held the bedrooms, including the master bedroom, two bedrooms used by the children, and the bedroom Martha's half-sisters used.

Is the house, or anywhere else on the property haunted? I got loads of information from the guide, but no other voices than hers, mine, and Bill's. No other noises out of the ordinary that I couldn't explain away. The photos were nice, but nothing strange about any of them. Neither the guide nor the docent in the office has ever had any paranormal experiences.

Though there have been stories about the place. Voices are heard, along with singing, and a man talking in the house when the place is quiet and they are alone. Patty Ceran herself has witnessed a door opening on its own. She has also heard that strange things happen to the townhouses next-door.

Take a tour of this lovely mansion. You might learn some history. Even more, you just might catch sight of history coming alive in a haunting way. It is located at 163 Yorktown Road in Newport News, not far from the Boxwood Inn and the Endview Plantation. For more information, plus directions, check out Lee Hall's website at www.leehall.org.

Lee Hall Mansion.

Outdoor kitchen of Lee Hall Plantation.

Civil War earthwork on Lee Hall property.

ENDVIEW PLANTATION

The Endview Plantation house came into view as we drove up the driveway and parked in the parking area allotted for the public. Not that far away from Lee Hall, tourists could combine checking out both places in one day, which I did on November 21, 2009. The museum is open Mondays, Wednesdays, Saturdays, and Sundays. It is closed Tuesday all year round and Wednesdays January 1- March 31. It does cost to take the tour.

In addition to the house, the property has two graveyards, a spring, and cabins that Civil War reenactors use when they do reenactments. The cemetery located across the field from the reenactors' cabins contains the mortal remains of the Harwood family — Humphrey Harwood, his wife, Lucy (who died in childbirth), and his sons, Daniel and Newton. Daughter Ellen is also buried there, plus others since the seventeenth century. The smaller grave site by the house itself has the Curtis children's graves.

Of course, with the difference in names one might think that the place had been owned by different families, but it hadn't. From 1622 until 1985 one family owned it. Thomas Harwood had landed at Jamestown after the 1622 Indian Massacre to join his uncle, Sir Edward Harwood, a Virginia Company stockholder, and his brother William. Thomas was joined by his wife, Grace. In 1626, he received a land grant of 100 acres. This is what Endview eventually would be built on.

William Harwood built the house in 1769 in the 'T'-frame Georgian-style. When he died in 1795, the large estate was divided. Endview went to one son, Humphrey, and Waterview on Mulberry Island was left to his other son, William, III. The Harwoods lived at Endview for ninety years. Abandoning tobacco as the staple crop, the Harwoods shifted to grains, other mixed crops, and cattle. Records show that the Harwood Plantation was home to between fifteen and twenty-five slaves between the Revolutionary War and the Civil War. Slave quarters were scattered around the vicinity of the house. There are references to a slave graveyard near the spring at one time. Having wooden markers, over time, the cemetery was lost.

In 1858, when Humphrey Harwood passed away, the property fell into his nephew, Dr. Humphrey Harwood Curtis's hands. A medical doctor, Curtis had taken classes at Jefferson Medical College in Philadelphia. At that time, you did not have to take classes to become a doctor — all you had to do is state it and practice it. However, Curtis did go to school to learn it. The young doctor established his medical practice at the plantation in 1856 and married Maria Whitaker in 1858. The 1860 census showed that Curtis owned $8,000 worth of real estate, $21,000 worth of personal property, and twelve slaves. It was also at this time that the name of the property changed to Endview. When the farm lane, which originally led to the north (back) side of the house, was moved, the dwelling was approached from the west end. Visitors were then greeted with an "end view."

Curtis passed away and was buried on what is Fort Eustis Golf Course today. At that time, it had been his family's interment grounds. His wife, Maria Curtis died in 1919 and is buried across the street from Endview at the church cemetery there. The property only passed from the family and became a rental in 1985, until the city of Newport News bought it in 1995. The house has been restored by the city to its 1862 appearance.

Dr. Curtis left practice and started a volunteer militia called the Warrick Beauregards (back then this was Warrick County, not York County today) to stop slaves from being free from Yankee interference. He was elected captain. Not one person in the militia had military experience and eventually a growing dissension among the militia led to an election that voted out Curtis. The Beauregards soon became Company H of the 32nd Virginia Volunteer Infantry Regiment and participated in the defense of the Peninsula before retreating with General Joseph Johnston's army May 3-4, 1862. Dr. Curtis took his wife and children and fled to Danville, Virginia, when the Siege of 1862 happened. There his doctoring was put in use as Danville was cut off, and pestilence and starvation erupted.

The Confederates used Endview for a brief time as a hospital. Northern troops also occupied the property. They remained in the area until the end of the war. The Federal government confiscated the plantation in early 1864, relocating seven African-American families there to farm it. The Curtis family did return after the war and within a few months regained possession of their property.

When Dr. Curtis passed away, Maria kept the place going by teaching piano to bring in money. It was the only way a genteel woman could earn a living back then. There had been a piano in the family that was received as a wedding gift, but when they returned, they did not have it. They'd gotten the one Maria used as payment for Dr. Curtis "doctoring" someone.

Endview Plantation House.

Smaller Curtis cemetery right by the house.

The Harwood Cemetery.

With all that happened here, surely the place had some paranormal stories to tell. Those who have visited the place claimed they heard voices and felt things. The docent who gave me the tour admitted that she never has, though. There are reports of a woman seen crossing the road from the cemetery towards the house during re-enactments that are held at the Plantation. Civil War re-enactors have complained of ghostly happenings in the cabins when they stay there for the reenactments, too. Doors open and close on their own, cold spots appear even in the summer, many of them felt a presence when they were alone and heard disembodied voices. Also a room used as a nursery has curtains that have been found open after they have been closed for the night. She was thinking about opening the place to paranormal investigators. I told her that would be great. Later, I heard when I interviewed the owner of Boxwood that the investigators that did her place also may have gone to Endview (interesting note: Dr. Curtis' son, Simon, was the one who built Boxwood).

It is thought from all accounts that maybe it is Maria who haunts the place. One time, a lady came to visit after her father died. Her mother had told her to go to Endview and see if it was her father who haunted the place. Of course, it wasn't. I think they had lived there once upon a time when it was a rental.

While on the tour, I took pictures and kept my digital recorder going. All I caught was the docent talking, but nothing out of the ordinary. No other voices other than hers and mine or unusual sounds I couldn't explain away. Same went for the photos. I admit though that later on, I did not feel as if I was alone at the cabins — I got a feeling of being watched. At this time, I did not know that the reenactors have had paranormal experiences there. Still, nothing more concrete.

The Endview is located at 362 Yorktown Road, Newport News. To find out when reenactments or special events are held, visit their website at http://www.endview.org/index.php.

SHARING A HOTEL ROOM WITH THE UNSEEN

A woman, Stephanie, had rented a room at a hotel in Newport News for her daughter and her. Her daughter got the pull out bed and she took the regular one. Most of the night passed uneventful for her. Until 5 a.m.

Something woke her up...something that sat on the bed, by her feet. She opened her eyes. The room was still dark, as the sun hadn't risen yet. Stephanie couldn't move. She tried to scream, but couldn't. Only her eyes moved, and she used them to search out what the problem was.

By her feet, sat a shadowy figure. It had red eyes and leaned towards her, staring at her. Frightened, Stephanie managed to move her hand to her leg, but that was it. She closed her eyes and knew that if she could just pinch her leg, she would wake up from this nightmare.

She opened her eyes again and noticed by the clock on the nightstand that four minutes had passed. The figure stood up and moved over to stand in the corner behind the clock. Much too close for her own comfort. Stephanie tried to scream again or shift a hand or foot. Anything. But nothing. So she shut her eyes.

Finally she could move a toe, then the foot, and the leg. She sat up and popped open her eyes. The dark figure was gone. Glancing at the clock, she saw it was 5:24 a.m. Her daughter still slept soundly in the pull out bed. Even better, rays of the sun filtered through the window, letting her know that dawn had arrived.

Stephanie turned on every light in the room. It was the scariest thing that ever happened to her. Definitely time to check out of the hotel.

Chapter Nine

HAMPTON

The city of Hampton is off of I-64 in the southeastern end of the Virginia Peninsula. Fort Monroe is located within its borders, along with Bluebird Gap Farm, the Virginia Air and Space Museum, Coliseum, Langley Air Force Base, NASA Langley Research Center, the Virginia Air and Space Center, and historic Hampton University.

Hampton is the oldest continuously settled English community in the United States. As an Indian village called Kecoughtan, it had been visited by the first English colonists before they sailed up the James River to settle in Jamestown.

The construction of Fort Henry and Fort Charles at the mouth of Hampton Creek in 1610 was the beginning of Hampton. The settlers chose an English name, Elizabeth City, in 1619, but it was known as Hampton as early as 1680. In 1705, it became recognized as a town. The City of Hampton was first incorporated in 1849 and classified as a city of the second class in 1908. In 1952, Hampton, the independent town of Phoebus, and Elizabeth City County, encompassing Buckroe and Foxhill, consolidated under one municipal government.

Hampton Coliseum

During the Civil War in 1861, the city was burned down by its own troops, as they did not want to surrender to the Federals. Before the fire, Hampton had thirty businesses and over one hundred homes, but fewer than six buildings remained intact after the fire. A fire besieged Hampton in 1884, sweeping through the downtown business district, almost destroying the area.

Today there are over 141,000 residents living in the bustling city. Even more so, there are those no longer alive that still haunt the city's homes, parks, and businesses.

Fort Monroe

You can find Fort Monroe by taking exit 268 off I-64. The fort was founded by Captain John Smith, who named it Old Point Comfort. There, the colonists would be able to see who entered the James River. It went through several name changes until it came to be called Fort Monroe, after the President James Monroe. It is the largest enclosed fortification in the United States. There are still oak trees that some tree experts say were probably present when Smith explored Old Point Comfort.

Interestingly, sometimes it is also called Fortress Monroe. Why that and not Fort Monroe? A fort is a fortification containing a garrison of troops. A fortress is a fortification enclosing a town within its walls. The latter type was popular in Europe and brought to highest development by Marshal Sebastien in the time of Louis XIV. In World War I, the term fortress applied to a town defended by detached forts surrounding it. However, Fort Monroe does not close and has never enclosed a town.

Fort Monroe had been designed by Brigadier General Simon Bernard. He happened to be the French military engineer and former aide to Emperor Napoleon I. Construction began in 1819 and ended in 1834. They called it Fortress Monroe at first, but then the Secretary of War sent out an order that it be called Fort Monroe and not Fortress Monroe. It wasn't easy to vanquish the Fortress part, though. The Post Office Department changed its name from Old Point Comfort to Fortress Monroe. Even more, one senator, William Mahone, tried in 1885 to get it changed back to Old Point Comfort. The military authorities objected to this last one, pointing out that the correct name was Fort Monroe. Finally, on November 15, 1941, the Post Office put an end to all the confusion by changing the name to Fort Monroe.

Fort Monroe's area includes the moat, which is sixty-three acres. The moat is one and one-quarter miles in circumference. The width ranges from 150 feet at the Main Sallyport to sixty feet at the East Gate. The moat is eight feet deep at high tide.

Built in a hexagon shape, the fort has bastions, which are pointed projections, and casemates that are rooms or chambers within walls designed to house 32-pounder cannons. The casemate guns were fired through embrasures (openings) in the wall. The museum on Fort Monroe is called Casemate Museum and is also haunted. I used my digital recorder and took pictures inside the museum — no EVPs or oddities in any of the photos.

Fort Monroe was one of the few forts not captured by the Confederates during the Civil War. During the war, it was an invincible base of operations for the Union Army and Navy, right in the heart of the Confederate territory. At the end of the war, Confederate President Jefferson Davis was held prisoner there for two years. He was falsely accused of plotting the assassination of President Abraham Lincoln and was placed in a hastily improvised cell in Casemate No. 2 on May 22, 1865. When you tour the Casemate Museum, you can peer through the same small barred window he stared through. In the outer room, once used by Union soldiers who guarded Davis, are relics from his captivity and exhibits that chronicle his life and career. Eventually, after four and a half months, Dr. Craven succeeded in getting Davis transferred to Carroll Hall, a brick building that used to stand in the northwest bastion of the fort, where the present guardhouse now is. Mrs. Davis obtained permission from President Johnson to stay at Fort Monroe near her husband. She stayed in a casemate, but General Henry S. Burton allowed her to move into Carroll Hall with Davis, along with her daughter, "Winnie," and Mrs. Davis' sister, Margaret Howell.

Some Native Americans were also held at Fort Monroe in 1833. These six Indians were led by Black Hawk, who had refused to recognize a treaty that made claims that his people had ceded all their land east of the Mississippi to the white men. A war ensued. What happened was a massacre when the white troops, aided by a gunboat, shot down all the Indians, including women and children. Black Hawk gave himself up at Fort Crawford, Prairie du Chien, in Wisconsin. He ended up in Washington D.C. by order to see President Andrew Jackson. He had them sent to Fort Monroe, feeling they could not escape from there. Black Hawk and the other Indians left Fort Monroe on the evening of June 4, 1833. After a bit of travel, they went back home.

Cell Jefferson Davis was imprisoned in at Fort Monroe.

African Americans stayed on Fort Monroe, not in capacity as prisoners, but seeking freedom from being slaves during the early stage of the Civil War. On orders from the War Department, General Butler sheltered and fed the fugitives and put the able-bodied ones to work. Serving as cooks, teamsters, laborers, carpenters, and stevedores, they received rations and a small monthly wage. Others made an independent living by oystering, fishing, and peddling. Still others served as guides and scouts for the Union Army. Butler called them "contraband": so many of them sought refuge at the fort that they were diverted into many "contraband camps." One, called Slabtown because the huts were made of slabs, was located northeast of the area that is now known as Phoebus. Schools were built at the fort. One famous African American that stayed on Fort Monroe was Harriet Tubman. Due to her leading hundreds of black people to freedom in the North in the years before the War Between the States, she was called the "Moses of her People."

Edgar Allan Poe

Enlisting in the United States Army under an assumed name, Edgar A. Perry, Poe's unit was first sent to Fort Moultrie, South Carolina, but eventually, the company was transferred to Fort Monroe. Poe was promoted to sergeant major on January 1, 1829. This was the highest rank an enlisted man could obtain, but he now wanted to get out of the army. He wanted to become a writer again. He wrote his foster father, John Allan, asking for help. He actually sent two more letters after the first one. John Allan ignored all three. It was when Poe's foster mother passed away on February 28, 1829, that Allan invited Poe to Richmond. They reconciled and Allan agreed to pay a substitute to complete Poe's term of enlistment. Poe was discharged from Fort Monroe on April 15, 1829. He had served almost two years of his five-year enlistment. Sergeant Samuel Graves served out the rest of Poe's enlistment for a fee of seventy-five dollars.

Edgar Allan Poe exhibit at Casemate Museum.

Poe did return to Old Point Comfort. He spent Sunday, September 9, 1849 at the Hygeia Hotel (the Champlain Hotel is the name now) with some friends. He was due to lecture in Norfolk that coming week. That evening, though, Poe recited his poetry on the hotel's veranda in the moonlight, including "The Raven," "Annabel Lee," and "Ulalume." Four weeks later Poe died at Washington College Hospital in Baltimore, Maryland.

Quarter No. 1

The oldest house at the fort; Lafayette once stayed in it overnight in 1824 when he toured the fort. U.S. President Lincoln stayed in it during his visit to Fort Monroe from May 6-11, 1862.

Almost as old are Buildings No. 17 and 18, opposite the Casemate Museum. Robert E. Lee, lieutenant of engineers at the fort, lived in the west half of the top floor of 17 from 1831-1834.

The house where Robert E. Lee lived on Fort Monroe is behind the sign.

Old Point Comfort lighthouse.

Old Point Comfort Lighthouse

Built in 1862, the lighthouse is still in active service today. As for the Casemate Museum, it serves as the Army's Coast Artillery Museum. Its programs deal with the history of Fort Monroe, Old Point Comfort, and the Coast Artillery Corps. It is, like I said earlier, haunted.

The abundant ghost stories about this place include those concerning Edgar Allan Poe, Ulysses S. Grant, Lafayette, Jefferson Davis, Abraham Lincoln, and Captain John Smith. Also ordinary ghosts and a luminous lady have been seen.

The Moat

There's also a legend that the moat contains a water monster that is said to be a relative of the Loch Ness Monster of Scotland. There are claims that the moat monster has been sighted, but no one has been able to determine what it really is. Maybe it is another version of Chessie, Virginia's own sea serpent sighted in the Chesapeake Bay and the Appomattox River in Hopewell.

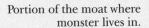
Portion of the moat where monster lives in.

When my husband and I visited the fort on Saturday, January 2, 2010, we didn't see an inkling of anything in the waters of the moat. Is it really a large sting ray or skate that became trapped in the moat during high tide one day and mistaken for a monster? More likely, just a figment of the imagination of soldiers and sailors stationed there.

The Ghost Stories

Regardless of whether the monster in the moat is real, it is said that ghosts haunt the various places on the fort, including the Casemate Museum and the Champlain Hotel. Jefferson Davis supposedly haunts his cell at Casemate No. 2. Is this an intelligent haunting where the spirit acknowledges you or a residue haunting because he had been imprisoned there?

Confederate ghosts have also been sighted there. One appeared in front of security guard, freaking him out enough to spill his coffee on himself! An employee, who worked in the museum's gift shop the day Bill and I were there, admitted that though she has never seen anything, she feels something when she walks through the place at closing time. It always unnerves her.

The house that Robert E. Lee lived in during his stay is said to be haunted. Toys move with no one living moving them and people hear heavy footsteps when no one mortal has made them. Pots and pans in the kitchen rattle and plates are smashed, drawers yanked open to spill utensils, and cabinet doors open and close with no human hand doing so. Elsewhere flowers have been torn out of vases and the petals scattered. A ghost child is blamed for using a box of discarded toys found in a basement — the toys are taken out and scattered about as if played with.

Another home on the fort has spirits due to a terrible tragedy concerning a love triangle; an officer, his wife, and another man. The husband was jealous and prone to anger. The wife fell in love with another man. The husband found out and one day snuck into the lover's place and shot his wife and her lover. It is she who is called the Luminous Lady seen behind the alley of the officer's quarters.

The Champlain Hotel also has its supernatural phenomena. It was built on the site of the earlier Hygeia hotel. The Hygeia offered a place of elegance to stay on Fort Monroe. With a ballroom, an on-site ice plant, laundry, billiards, a bowling alley, and electricity, the rich and politically powerful chose it as the place to stay. The Hygeia was torn down and the hotel built in its place burned down in the 1920s, then the Champlain was built in the same spot. It had much of what the Hygeia had, plus amenities that included a fitness room and a swimming pool.

The ghost that haunts the place is a woman on the eighth floor. The legend goes that her name was Esmeralda who worked as a chambermaid for the hotel and was married to a poor fisherman. Though poor, they were happy. One day, her husband did not return from a fishing trip. She waited for him, staring out the window. The manager caught her doing so and fired her. At the same time, a fire broke out in the kitchen and spread through the hotel. Many were saved, but others weren't, including Esmeralda and some of the staff. Apparently trapped on the eighth floor where the smoke was the worst, her wraith is said to hang around. So frightened were those who beheld her, that the manager would not rent any rooms on that floor. She has been seen floating past while others complain of cold spots. Still others feel an intense heat in her presence.

Though I never got to talk to the man who was the expert on the spirits of Fort Monroe and lived in the Champlain, I did used the restroom on the second floor before I left to go to the Casemate Museum. After a woman left the room, I decided to test out my new KII EMF Meter that I had gotten for Christmas. I asked if anyone was in the place and if so, to make the second light come on. It did. I asked if it could make the third one come one. The third light did. Excited, I asked that whomever shared the restroom with me would make the fourth light blink on. That's when all the lights went off, except the first one. Was that Esmeralda? Or someone else? I'll never know. I used the digital recorder too, but there was nothing caught on audio.

Due to heightened security on bases after 9/11, the Champlain closed as a hotel from bankruptcy. Bought later, the new owners renovated the place and made it into luxury apartments for senior citizens. The place lives on — and maybe, if you peer up at the eighth floor, you just might see a woman's face peering out a window, searching for a beloved husband that never came home.

Come September 2011, pursuant to a decision by the 2005 Base Realignment and Closure Commission (BRAC), the Army will vacate Fort Monroe. Most of the property will revert to the Commonwealth of Virginia, and as host city, Hampton, will play a role in its future.

Champlain Hotel.

Part of second floor of the hotel.

BLUEBIRD GAP FARM

Bluebird Gap Farm offers an exciting, family-oriented adventure and educational experience rarely seen in an urban environment. The sixty-acre farm has more than 250 domestic and wild animals, including everything from the usual array of farm animals to a bobcat, raccoons, birds of prey, whitetail deer, tortoises, and peacocks. A shelter with four picnic tables and charcoal grill is available on a first come, first served basis.

Visitors will enjoy the Hampton Master Gardeners' Display Garden and Arboretum, a large playground, a nature trail, and a new stage with seating for special events and activities. Admission is free. The park is open Wednesday through Sunday from 9 a.m. to 5 p.m. and closed on all major holidays except Easter. To find the park, take the I-64 exit 263B onto Mercury Boulevard. Turn right onto Coliseum Drive, follow to the stoplight, and take a right onto Pine Chapel Road. The farm is on the left, located at 60 Pine Chapel Road.

Bluebird Gap Farm was originally located on the site of the Hampton Coliseum. It opened there in 1966 and was then named "Old MacDonald's Farm." Redeveloped at its current location in 1969, the farm also has ghosts. There have been incidents of people being lightly touched and two different people have seen a young boy and an old man in overalls disappear. The witness saw the old man walk across the wooded area towards the parking lot. A delivery truck was the only vehicle parked there at the time because the park was closed. The man went behind the truck and never came out on the other side.

Patty Ceran sent me an e-mail about some paranormal experiences she and her grandson, Cody Dodson, had at the park. It was she who found the information that the place had been part of a plantation where the Hampton Coliseum now stands. She received copies of the land deeds and a list of who is buried in the graves.

Entrance to Bluebird Gap Farm.

Davis Graveyard

Mr. Davis is one of those buried there. He served in the Civil War and, after the war ended, came home to farm. He was in the fields checking on his workers and then went into his house to eat lunch when he died from a heart attack. Patty's gut instinct is this is the ghost wearing the overalls, as she felt a farmer in the later 1800s would wear those.

Patty never saw the man and was not sure if he was the same man that her grandson saw, but she did know that Cody talked to and played with someone unseen that day. He also saw a lady in the woods, too. The female ghost wore a long blue dress.

Patty has been back to Bluebird Gap Farm with her grandson and his mother lately. They took Cody there for the first time since the summer of 2009. Patty asked if it was all right if they visited the graves. Cody said sure and that was where he saw the lady. They walked back there when he stopped at the edge of the path and pointed to the trees where he had seen the ghost lady for the first time.

"That is where I saw the lady in the mask," he said.

His mother asked him why he thought she wore a mask. Cody said that her face looked different. Patty wanted to know why she looked different to him.

"She just looked different than we do, like she was not all there," he replied.

Patty explained to him again that he saw what people call a spirit and that sometimes they look different from living people. She also said that not everyone could see them and that he had a very special gift. He seemed satisfied with this explanation and ran over to the gate. He entered and walked up to the grave stone of Alice. He told Patty that was the lady he saw that day.

Davis graveyard on Bluebird Gap Farm.

Philip Davis's gravestone.

Cody then wandered over to the grave of Phillip and said that he had seen him, too. Patty asked if this was the papa that he had seen that day and walked with. Cody said "Yes." Patty also wondered if this was the man who wanted to take him out in the boat and Cody told her yes again. This took her by surprise because he had not mentioned "the papa" again since the day he saw him.

Bill and I visited the park on May 21, 2010. When we arrived, we found lots of children with their parents entering the park. We parked our car and left it to enter the park. Just as we did a school bus stopped and unloaded children with adults, all for a field trip, no doubt.

We saw animals and birds, mainly those found on farms, though there was a deer, raccoon, and barn owl, too. There were signs that indicated mountain lions, bobcats, and wolves, but we found these had passed away long ago and were never replaced as predators had to have a special license that cost a lot and the city didn't want to pay to renew it.

I got directions to the Davis cemetery and walked past the rabbit enclosure, strolled past some Canadian geese resting on the grass by a pond, and found a sign pointing to where the gravesite would be back in the woods. The cemetery lay next to what looked like a river or a lake. I took some snapshots of the whole cemetery, the graves, and nearby woods. I also recorded to see if I could capture any EVPs. It was growing hot and muggy, and the place seemed quiet and nothing out of the ordinary. Finally I joined Bill and we left the park to meet a friend for lunch before driving to find the Moore House.

Sometimes parks are more than a place for fun activities. Just like the living, ghosts like to enjoy parks, too.

OTHER GHOSTLY ENCOUNTERS

Still Pulling Teeth?

It seems that even dentists after death still come back to their places of employment. As so happens at the dental office at 1420 King Street in Hampton, where a former dentist committed suicide in the 1970s. When a new dentist took the office over, employees would sense the dead man's presence and even heard the drill being used when no one was.

When a clairvoyant came there one day, she said that the spirit wanted his mother to know that he did not kill himself. He just liked to use nitrous oxide (laughing gas) and one night at the office had overdosed.

Haunted dentist office.

Ghostly Presence at Fernandez Studio

A ghost likes to peep over employees' shoulders, just to see what they are doing at the time. He has been seen since the 1970s and mostly prefers the darkroom to anywhere else in the portrait studio.

Interestingly enough, when Bill and I found the building, we found that the Fernandez Studio was no longer there and that store was up for rent. Had the ghost chased them away?

Fernandez Studio is no longer in this strip mall, but the storefront is for rent.

Dead Firemen Don't Stay Dead

It seems you can't keep a good firefighter down, even after death. Phoebus Fire Station at 122 Hope Street has a firefighter called Fire Engine Charlie that opted to stay at his old fire station instead of going over to the other side. He has been heard walking upstairs and even playing pool in the game room, but does he go on calls when the engine is called out?

Phoebus Fire Station.

She Saw Her Friend's Grandfather

A woman and her best friend both lived in Hampton as children. When they were thirteen or fourteen, she spent the night at her friend's home. Both went downstairs late at night to get a snack and were talking in the kitchen when it happened. The girl glanced up and saw a strange man watching her.

He was a thin, older man who was almost bald and wore a button-down shirt, slacks, and sweater vest. She looked away and when she turned back, found he had vanished. She dismissed the whole thing as a dream.

About six months later her friend pulled out a shoebox that she kept pictures in. Both girls searched through them when the girl stopped to stare at one that reminded her of the man she saw at the top of the stairs, only he wasn't so skinny and had more hair. She told her friend, who produced another picture of the same man when he was older. He looked exactly like he did that night. The man was her grandfather who had lost weight and passed away due to complications from cancer.

Chapter Ten

THE POWHATAN AND POCAHONTAS

"Treat the earth well: it was not given to you by your parents, it was loaned to you by your children. We do not inherit the Earth from our Ancestors, we borrow it from our Children." — Tribe Unknown

Before the first white settlers touched ground in Virginia, the Algonquian lived in Virginia. One of the Algonquian tribes is the Powhatan. If you know the story of Pocahontas and John Smith, then you know that she came from this tribe. When the first white settlers landed, they were the most powerful of all the Algonquian tribes. There were thirty different tribes of Indians in the Powhatan Confederacy, 10,000 when the colonists arrived in Virginia. The Algonquian lived mainly around the Chesapeake Bay and its surrounding rivers.

The Powhatan built their homes out of saplings. There was a hole at the top of each frame, so that smoke could escape from their fires as they kept a fire going all of the time. Most people would imagine that this was for cooking or warmth, but they did this due to a superstition. It was believed that evil spirits would enter their homes if their fires died.

There is a legend connected to Powhatan not set in the Historic Triangle area, but in nearby Richmond. It concerns the "Powhatan Stone." The legend says that the Powhatan Seat is supposed to be where Tree Hill Farm is now, a mile or so outside of Richmond city limits on Route 5. There are other stories that say otherwise, that Powhatan ruled from what is now known as Fulton Hill. The Stone itself can be viewed just outside the Chimborazo Hospital Museum in Church Hill, overlooking Bloody Run.

POCAHONTAS

Pocahontas lived in the Historic Triangle area when the first white settlers came. Born around 1595, she was the daughter of Wahunsunacock (also known as Chief or Emperor Powhatan) and one of his many wives. Her father ruled the Algonquian Indians in Werawocomoco (what is now Wicomico, Gloucester County, Virginia). Her name meant "Little Wanton," or a playful, frolicsome little girl.

When the English colonists landed in May 1607, Pocahontas was most likely ten or eleven years old, not like in the Disney animated film. The first legendary meeting of Pocahontas and John Smith is romanticized, if not entirely invented, by Smith himself.

Leading an expedition in December 1607, Smith was captured by Indians and brought to the official residence of Powhatan at Werawocomoco. In Smith's version of the tale, the great chief welcomed him and offered him a feast, but then the braves grabbed him and stretched him out on two large, flat stones. They stood over him with clubs and it looked like they were going to beat him to death. Just at that point, a little girl ran up to him, took his head in her arms, and laid hers upon his. This saved him from death. This was Pocahontas. She helped him to his feet and that was when Powhatan acknowledged him as a friend and even adopted Smith as his son, or a subordinate chief. In actuality, the mock "execution and salvation" ceremony was traditional among the Indians at that time. If what happened was true, what Pocahontas did was part of a ritual.

On a website owned by Chief Roy Crazy Horse, it was seventeen years after the fact that John Smith told his tale. Time could have caused distortions in what really happened that day. In the original account Smith wrote after his winter stay with Powhatan's people, he never mentioned the incident. He said that he had been kept comfortable and treated as an honored guest of Powhatan and Powhatan's brothers. It was after he met Pocahontas years later and saw how the royalty of England thought of her that he rewrote his story to include Pocahontas saving his life.

Most scholars think the "Pocahontas incident" would have been highly unlikely, especially since it was part of a longer account used as justification to wage war on Powhatan's Nation. Pocahontas married John Rolfe, another Jamestown colonist, at Citie of Henricus and had a son, Tomas, and then traveled to England with some other Indians. When she encountered Smith there (whom she obviously thought was dead as that was what she had been told when he returned to England years before), she turned her back on him, hid her face, and went off by herself.

Another myth, mostly told in movies, though some stories too, that there was a love between her and Smith. This is a myth. Since she was maybe 10 or 11 years old, she would have been too young to think of love with a much older white man.

There's another small possible myth connected with Pocahontas — that she might have been married to an Indian man before she married John Rolfe. I found a reference to her marrying Kocoum, a "captain" of her father's tribe. Now it could be the truth as she was absent from the colony for a few years, but it is just as possible that the nickname Pocahontas ("playful" or "willful" one) also applied to another daughter of Powhatan. The source says the one who married Kocoum was "Pocahuntas...rightly called Amonate." Was Amonate another daughter of Powhatan, or did Pocahontas (real name Matoaka) have yet another name?

Throughout her short life until she died of smallpox at age twenty-two, Pocahontas helped her people in a most important way by bringing peace between the Powhatans and the English colonists. Captain Samuel Argall captured her in 1613 and held her at the fort for a year as part of a bargaining deal with her father. During this time, she converted to Christianity, baptized to the name, Rebecca.

She married John Rolfe, a union which helped bring the two groups together. Sadly, just as John Rolfe was about to take his family home to Virginia, she fell ill and died. Her body is buried at Gravesend, Kent in England still to this day. She is recorded: "1616 March 21, Rebecca Rolfe, Wyffe of Thomas John Rolfe Gentleman, a Virginia Lady borne was buried in ye chancell. Entered by Rev. Nicholas Frankwell."

A sad ending to a great story.

MATOAKA ALS R..

VIRGINIa.

POWHATANI IMP:

..LIA POTENTISS: PRINC:

Ætatis suæ 22. Ao
1616

ocahontas,
in London.
s after she
fe in 1614.

..alias Rebecca, 1616
Richmond, Virginia

Pocahontas picture from inside Jamestown Memorial Church.

Section Three:

OTHER PHENOMENA
IN THE HISTORIC TRIANGLE

Chapter Eleven
THE COHOKE LIGHT

They say a spectral light is seen in West Point, Virginia. It has been seen by many and no one knows what really causes the haunting, though there are two legends behind it. One of these tales concerns a conductor who was walking along the tracks, lantern in hand, when a train whipped past him. A chain hanging off the train swung from it and separated his head from his neck. Some people claim to have seen him walking along the tracks, swinging his lantern back and forth, as he searches for his head. Mostly though, witnesses just catch sight of a bobbing white light. There are claims that it will follow you to Churchville Road and then disappear. Others claim that you will see it in front of you and then it races through you to hover behind you. There are those who believe it is real while others theorized it is swamp gas, or spirits of the alcoholic kind, rather than supernatural. Most sightings seem to be on dismal nights, mainly cloudy or rainy.

The light has been seen for a hundred years in the Tidewater region. It became a cool thing for teenagers to drive up to the site, hoping to catch sight of it. A good author friend of mine, Deborah Painter, and her sister did that when both were younger.

At one point in the 1960s and 1970s, one King William County sheriff, W. W. Healey, called it a circus, with crowds of people milling around the area. He even had to say no to NBC's "Unsolved Mysteries" request to film there. Though it has died down, the sheriff never went down there, more from fear of those who take guns with them to shoot at anything resembling a light. When my husband and I found the spot, there were no other people, just silent woods on either side of the tracks.

Another legend of what the light could be is of a lost train. Not long after the battle of Cold Harbor, wounded Confederate soldiers boarded a train in Richmond. The train rolled along the tracks to West Point, but apparently never reached its destination. Like a ghost, the entire train with the men just vanished, with no explanation.

An interesting footnote to this legend is what happened to Tom Gulbranson of Oceanview and his family in 1967. They went there because Tom was an amateur psychic sleuth. He had visited the Cohoke site many times and seen the light on several occasions. The particular night in question was a freezing cold one. Nothing happened, so he packed up his camera equipment to leave — and that's when the light appeared, brighter than he had ever seen it before. The occupants from the car parked next to them flicked on their headlights. Startled, Tom saw the outline of a train in the light.

One witness, Walt Gruner of Penns Grove, New Jersey, who used to live in Virginia and is planning to return, sent me an e-mail of his experience with the Cohoke Light. Back in the 1960s, with several of his friends from Northumberland County, he made the trip once or twice a month to the area to see the light. The location was in a swampy area between two roads, maybe a mile or two apart. Nothing but woods, it was very dark also. Sometimes they saw it, while other times nothing happened.

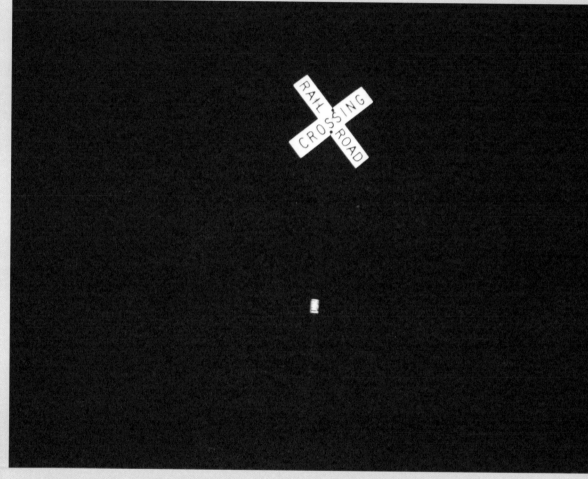

Mt. Olive Cohoke Road railroad crossing at night. This is where the Cohoke Light has been seen.

One night, only four or five of them trekked down to the spot. The light did show up. Now Walt admitted that being young and two sheets to the wind, he dared the others to walk down the tracks to it. The others chickened out and he said he took off by himself, being some kind of a macho thing at the time, and with enough liquid bravery coursing through his veins. One guy, Les, changed his mind about not going and decided to join Walt. With only the light and the tracks to guide them, the young men trampled on. The liquid bravery soon wore off. They grew even a little bit frightened for there was not only the light, but noises from denizens of the swamp.

It seemed that at times they got closer to the light while other times it kept its distance. They kept walking and Walt suspected the tracks curved because they couldn't see anything behind or in front of them. With no moon that night, the place was pitch black, making it hard to see. Les was behind Walt a step or two, when all of a sudden they heard a splash in the water right beside them. Walt jumped when something grabbed his shoulder. He snapped his head around and found a shaken Les had a death grip on his shoulder.

They composed themselves as much as they could and continued on. At that point Walt realized the light no longer was ahead of them. Turning around, he saw that it now hovered behind them, at what they thought was the same proximity to them when it had been in front. They bolted back to their friends waiting for them at the second road. The friends had been about to panic, thinking something must had happened to them. After that particular episode, Walt no longer had any further interest in future midnight swamp walks to search for the light.

Seeing the Light?

On January 2, 2010, Bill and I swung off I-64 onto the off ramp that said West Point and, using our GPS, we drove for twenty minutes before we found the general area and Churchville Road. We turned onto it and rolled past homes along Churchville.

The train tracks and crossing signals appeared suddenly amidst darkened woods on both sides. The only light came from the headlights and the full moon above. Bill drove over the crossing and swung around to park off road, not far from the crossing. I will admit that he wasn't happy as it was late and there was a movie he wanted to see at nine o'clock. Plus he worried about a police car coming along and finding us there, maybe even giving us a ticket or chasing us off. It is illegal to park near the tracks like this, but I told him we would make it home in time and besides, we had set the DVR to record it just in case. Plus I wouldn't be long, only a few minutes.

I climbed out of the car with my pink bookbag of equipment slung over one shoulder and my camera hung around my neck. I felt the bone-chilling cold air just like at Crawford Road earlier that night, though I swore it seemed to have grown much colder. Plus it was pitch dark, with the only light coming from a full moon above. But the night sky was also clear and along with the full moon, stars scattered across its velvet shadow. I got close to the crossing and stared down the tracks, first to my right, then to my left. No light appeared to welcome me. Of course, the legends said that the light showed up on rainy or cloudy nights. Though what happened to Tom Gulbranson was on a freezing night, so maybe I would still have luck.

I took my KII EMF meter out of the bookbag and pushed it on. At first, I got nothing. Then all the lights came on and turned off just as quickly. After that, nothing for the rest of the time. Okay, that was weird. I learned later that doesn't happen normally.

Did I catch the Cohoke Light over the tracks, besides orbs?

I turned it off and put it away. Next came out my digital recorder. I clicked it on.

"Is there anyone here? If there is and you want to talk to me, talk into my recorder."

I let it go for a while and looked around, even walking up the tracks. I knew my husband was anxious, but I had to do this.

Finally I came back and shut the recorder off, putting it away. That was when I began snapping shots all around the area. With that done and knowing my husband waited for me, I headed back to the car and got in. We drove straight home. By the way, we made it home just as the movie started.

The next day, I listened to my recordings of the Cohoke Light area and Crawford Road. Like at Crawford, I had caught something. Nothing as eerie as Crawford, but it was strange nevertheless. I heard myself talking and then nothing but silence for a while. Suddenly, what sounded like a rushing wind came out of the recorder. After a few seconds of that peculiar sound, it went back to the silence.

Was that maybe the ghost of the Civil War train passing by, or something else? There was no wind or even a small breeze that night, just stillness. I did capture some orbs in one photo, along with what looks like a tiny light right over the tracks. Some might point out that maybe it was a bug, but this was in January, during a freezing cold night. Had I capture the Light on camera?

Another one had what looked like twin red eyes staring at me from a patch of woods across the tracks that could be explained away as a deer or some other animal, but the picture still looked creepy.

Whatever was there that night for me, I can't say for sure what that light thing was, or even what that sound like the wind on my recorder was. I did get some food for thought, though. Maybe another time I will attempt to go back there, with some fellow investigators.

Next time you decide you'll park near the crossing and walk alongside the tracks on a dark night, just be careful. Especially if a glowing light starts coming toward you. It just might be someone looking for his head, or a train lost in time.

Chapter Twelve

BIGFOOT ENCOUNTERS

"Behind every tree there's a new monster."
— Todd Rundgren

Virginia has the oldest records of Sasquatch sightings in the United States, with some dating back to the pre-1880s. The Department of Forestry's website mentions about 15.8 million acres of forest in the state, with sixty-two percent of Virginia owned by private citizens. Sightings of this creature have been reported to this day, some of them by credible people. The facts suggest some kind of animal, even a primate, but being bipedal, unlike an ape, it struts with long strides, has a conical top of the head, and is adept at avoiding human contact. Many maintain they have seen a Sasquatch while others say these sightings are misidentification of bears, wishful thinking, and deliberate fabrication of evidence.

Various websites (like the Sasquatch Watch of Virginia), blogs, and books have pinpointed sightings all over Virginia, from near Washington D.C. to the Shenandoah Valley, from Roanoke to Richmond and its counties, and as far south as the North Carolina border and as far east as the Tidewater region. With many stories of wildlife observed in people's very own backyards or trotting down city streets, has the encroachment of human habitation on what once was stretches of country made it possible for us to catch views of Sasquatch, too?

There are a couple of tales of Bigfoot reported in the Historic Triangle area, one in York County and the other in Hampton. It seems that history can't scare away these big lumbering creatures.

In April 2005, Bill was driving down I-64 in York County with his wife and sister when a large ape-like creature covered in red hair or fur suddenly bounded across the lanes of the freeway in the daytime. Three cars besides his screeched to a halt down the road from them. It stopped and turned around, placing a paw on the window of a red car and stared at the cars. It then shambled away and headed into the woods off the road, but it paused for a second just before disappearing and looked back at them, with what Bill said looked like dignity. It entered the woods. Bill was upset that he didn't have a camera at the time for such an opportunity.

The next time someone sighted a Sasquatch happened around Hampton in June of 2002, by a witness who wished to remain anonymous. The event was centered near Salt March Back River. The witness was walking with his brothers, looking for a place to do some fishing. It was about 6:30 p.m. and the sun was setting — that was when they saw the creature. The witness figured it stood about eight feet tall and was covered in reddish-brown hair all over. It clumped away from them, its arms swinging. Two days later, a black bear was caught by the city, but the witness knew that was not what they saw. For what they had caught sight of had reddish-brown hair, not black.

So next time you drive down Route 5 in Charles City late at night or even lonely stretches of roads with woods on both sides in Williamsburg or York County, be on the lookout for something large running in front of your vehicle. Don't stop. Just keep going. For if you look back, you just might see a large hairy being standing at the edge of the woods, staring after you. For more than ghosts and wildlife can inhabit the woods.

Chapter Thirteen

UFOS AMONG US

"You know what happens to most people after seeing a UFO?" — "The X-Files"

The past couple books I've written didn't contain any UFO stories. I decided to do so in this book.

UFO means unidentified flying object. Though it is said since the 1940s there have been sightings, some documented, some not, there is no doubt that since man first walked the earth such objects have been seen in the skies. There have been suspicions that some text in the Bible and many mythologies could be referring to UFOs or even alien contact.

The modern history of UFOs, though, perhaps begins in 1947 with an Idaho businessman and pilot named Kenneth Arnold. As he flew near Mount Rainier in the state of Washington, Arnold spotted a formation of nine silvery crescent-shaped objects flying in tight formation. Later on, he figured that they were forty to fifty feet wide, with their speed hitting at a fantastic 1,200 miles per hour, more than twice as fast as any known aircraft of that time. He described the movements to a reporter as "like pie plates skipping over the water." The reporter coined the term "flying saucers" the next day, and the label stuck.

After that, UFO sightings in our skies exploded. On June 26, four witnesses saw a "huge silver globe" moving along the rim of the Grand Canyon. Not long after that, about two days, an Air Force pilot reported a sighting of six discs over Lake Meade, Nevada. Reports came rushing in from places like Michigan, Ohio, Oregon, Louisiana, Quebec, and Prince Edward Island in far-north Canada.

From 1952 on, UFO sightings piled up for months. Most came from airline and military pilots. An Air Force report declassified in 1985 describes radar sightings involving up to twelve unidentified "targets" at a time near Washington National Airport. At a large peacetime press conference, the Air Force attributed the radar activity to "temperature inversions," but local meteorologists said it was not. What do you think?

The most infamous story has to do with Roswell, New Mexico, and the crash landing of one of these UFOs. On July 2, 1947, a farmer, Mac Brazel, heard a loud crash during a thunderstorm. The next day, when he was out riding with his neighbors to check on his sheep, he found debris scattered in the field. The debris on the field mostly consisted of I-beams and parchment-like, paper-thin pieces of metal material. The material was very light in weight, colored dull gray, and most of the pieces were six to seven inches in length. Some pieces that were even thinner than paper could not be broken in half, cut, or burned. Mac picked up several pieces of the stuff and went back to his ranch. The next day, he reported it to the local sheriff, who in turn, contacted Roswell Army Air Field. Not long after, Major Jesse Marcel and others from the 509th Bomb group arrived and went to the field with Brazel. Marcel gathered up some of the debris, even stopping at his home on the way to the base, to drop some pieces off.

On July 8, 1947, a press release went out that the wreckage of a crashed disk had been recovered. This was issued by the Commander of the 509th Bomb Group at Roswell, Colonel William Blanchard. At 11 a.m. Walter Haut, public relations officer, finished the press release he'd been ordered to write and gave copies of the release to the two radio stations and both of the newspapers. By 2:26 p.m., the story was announced on the AP Wire: "The Army Air Forces here today announced a flying disk had been found." Calls began to pour into the base from all over the world. It was not long after that began happening that the flying saucer turned into a balloon and the details became murky. Supposedly, the air base is sealed off, Brazel got taken into custody, and military police closed some roads.

The same day, it is said that a second crash site was discovered two and half miles southeast of the first. Barney Barnett and 4 archaeologists had stumbled onto the new site only a few minutes before the military got there. At the site they pretended they had found a "pretty good sized metallic dull gray object" and four small alien bodies. The bodies were about four to five feet tall, had large pear shaped heads, small bodies, and skinny arms and legs. They had two large eyes, no ears and no hair, with leathery, pinkish-gray skin. The aliens wore one-piece grey suits. The civilians were escorted out of the area and MPs carried loaded wreckage onto a C-54 from the First Transport Unit. Then it was taken back to base.

It was after that the now famous photo of Marcel with the weather balloon came to light and the story of his discovery not being a spacecraft was told. There have been books written about this and a senator even had the case reopened for investigation.

For years, there have been the Air Force Blue Book, crop circles, close encounter stories, alien abductions and more, all starting from the first sighting of a flying saucer. Virginia has had them as much as any other state in the United States. And some of them have been in the Historic Triangle and Charles City area.

In Gloucester County, one witness saw two round-looking objects with a line running through each one on the sides, thinking they were something like wings. He figured that the objects were traveling pretty fast, when the one in the front took off and flew like faster than the other one. It moved so fast that he knew it couldn't be any other type of aircraft that he knew of. Figured it had to have been an UFO.

The next person to see an UFO was in Hampton. He had been on Mercury Boulevard, heading toward the Hampton Coliseum. His father, brother, friend and he were going to the theater to see the movie "Stargate." When they turned onto Mercury Blvd. his friend saw a "thing" hovering in the distance. When he himself looked up, to his shock he saw something like a huge cylinder floating in the distance. It reflected the afternoon sun. Even though he figured it had to be massive, it looked to be about a mile high up in the sky. They watched it when they stopped at a stop light for about a minute and noticed people in other cars pointing at it and shaking their heads. They considered that it may be a balloon or even a military craft, but in the end, he decided it was an UFO.

The next sighting happened in Williamsburg. The witness said that his father worked at a major brewery in Williamsburg. He knew pretty much everyone who worked there and learned about this tale from one of the guys who saw it. Two truckers were behind the brewery loading their trucks at about 4 a.m., when one of them noticed something odd. They saw something reflecting the big flood lights coming around the corner. When it did, they saw a disc shape, hovering about twenty feet off the ground. They stopped packing the trucks and stared in astonishment. The object hovered for a few minutes, then drew closer to the men. It stopped suddenly and an appendage of some sort came out of the side and seemed to be inspecting them and their trucks. One of the men grabbed a flashlight from into his glove box. He shone the light right at it. The appendage just disappeared into the side of the disc. The men said it sat there for about ten minutes, so the one with the flashlight flashed it again. At that point, it turned and slowly hovered up and away until it was out of sight.

In 2009, a team of scientists looked into what could have caused bright lights in the sky that prompted hundreds of calls to the National Weather Service and emergency officials. This happened over Maryland, Virginia and North Carolina. The callers described brilliant, streaking lights and an explosion-like sound around 9:45 p.m. on Sunday, March 29th. Virginia residents from Hampton Roads to Richmond reported seeing "great balls of fire" that lit up the sky in yellow, white, orange and blue. Some described the explosion as sounding like thunder. The weather service claimed that no damage was reported. What was it? Some explanations said it was a meteor or debris from a Russian rocket booster. Was it so easily explained, or could it have been due to an UFO?

Whether you believe in UFOs or not, or even little gray men, the Historic Triangle area had sightings just like the rest of Virginia. Maybe even beings from another world just might be tourists themselves, interested in a part of Virginia where a part of U.S. history started.

CONCLUSION

Dear Readers, you've reached the last page. I hope you enjoyed the ghostly tales and legends that make up the Historic Triangle, Charles City, West Point, Hampton, Poquoson, Newport News, and Gloucester, and that you even learned some history along the way.

Whether it's Sasquatch, UFOs, ghosts, monsters, or even urban legends, this part of the Virginia Peninsula is chock full of such things. Next time you take a tour of Colonial Williamsburg or Yorktown, check out where the first colony was or even drive down creepy Crawford Road. Remember the area has more than history — it has the paranormal!

BIBLIOGRAPHY

Asfar, Dan. *Ghost Stories of Virginia*. Auburn, Washington: Lone Pine Publishing, International,1973.

Behrend, Jackie Eileen. *The Hauntings of Williamsburg, Yorktown, and Jamestown*. Winston-Salem, North Carolina: John F. Blair Publisher, 2006.

Hauck, Dennis William. *Haunted Places: The National Directory*. New York, New York: Penguin Books, 2002.

Hunter, John P. *Witches and Ghosts, Pirates and Thieves, Murder and Mayhem*. Williamsburg, Virginia: The Colonial Williamsburg Foundation, 2007.

Kelso, William M. *Jamestown: The Buried Truth*. Charlottesville, Virginia and London, England: University of Virginia Press, 2006.

Kinney, Pamela K. *Haunted Virginia: Legends, Myths, and True Tales*. Atglen, Pennsylvania: Schiffer Publishing, Ltd., 2007

Petretto, Cecilia. *Ghosts, Legends, and Lore of Hampton Roads*. Atglen, Pennsylvania: Schiffer Publishing, Ltd., 2010.

Taylor, L. B. *The Ghosts of Virginia Volume II*. Williamsburg, Virginia: L. B. Taylor, 1996.

Ghosts of Virginia Volume XII. Williamsburg, Virginia: L. B. Taylor, 2007.

The Ghosts of Williamsburg…and Nearby Environs. Williamsburg, Virginia: L. B. Taylor, 1983.

The Ghosts of Williamsburg II. Williamsburg, Virginia: L. B. Taylor, 1999.

Tucker, George H. *Virginia Supernatural Tales*. Norfolk, Virginia: The Donning Company/ Publishers, Inc., 1977.

INDEX